Cumber

Celebrating 100 years of service

Harry Postlethwaite

ISBN 978 1905 304 493

Computer Origination, Design and Layout by John Senior

FOREWORD

Cumberland Motor Services Ltd started its corporate life as Whitehaven Motor Service Company Ltd on 8th August 1912, changing the corporate name twice: on 1st June 1921 to Cumberland Motor Services Limited and again on 22nd May 1991 to Stagecoach (North West) Limited.

Whilst the name of the corporate entity may change, the principles of serving the people of Cumbria have not. Staff are as dedicated today as they ever have been in striving to maintain the best standards of customer service.

Road passenger transport operators continue to play a key role in minimising social and economic exclusion with increasing green credentials as vehicle investment and commercial innovation persuade car drivers onto the environmentally friendlier mode of transport, the bus.

This would not be possible without the commitment of staff, who have been challenged over the years to maintain customer service in the most difficult, and at times harrowing, of circumstances. The floods of 2005 and 2009 brought out the very best in staff and reminded us all of the dedication and professionalism that underpins this company.

In the Company's 100th year of service the pride, dedication and professionalism of staff is surely as strong today as it ever has been in the Company's long history.

With the continued new investment in vehicles the Company moves towards its centenary facing many challenges ahead but confident in the people who support and deliver the services vital to the people of Cumbria.

Nigel Winter. Managing Director, Stagecoach Cumbria and North Lancashire

To celebrate the centenary of Cumberland Motor Services, Alexander-Dennis Dart SLF Pointer 2, PX05 ENE (Stagecoach fleet No. 34702) was painted in the style of that company. Here it is swinging into Botchergate, Carlisle on 12th April 2012 on the 67 Belle Vue - Upperby route. (DMcA)

1. *Before the Motor Buses.*

One of the earliest references to public transport in West Cumberland was an advertisement in the Whitehaven Gazette dated Thursday 25th March 1897. This was placed by the Whitehaven Cab and General Posting Company announcing that they had 'Commenced running a bus which will meet all trains'. Orders from any part of the town were assured of prompt attention. No further evidence relating to the operation of this service has been traced.

At this time tramways were being developed in many parts of the country. The West Cumberland Electric Tramways Company, based in Whitehaven, was authorised by Act of Parliament in 1901, to build an ambitious system. It was to be of 4ft 8½ins. gauge with a route length of 31¼ miles extending from Cleator Moor via Hensingham Square, Whitehaven, Distington, Workington, Low Seaton, Gillhead, Flimby, Maryport, Allonby, Beckfoot to Silloth. The proposal included 12¾ miles of reserved track. Perhaps it was just too ambitious and it was never built. Just imagine the delight of travelling by tramcar along the coast road between Maryport and Silloth. Blackpool could never have compared with that!

~~~~~~~~~~~~~~

Public Notices.

~~~~~~~~~~~~~~

WHITEHAVEN CAB & GENERAL POSTING CO., LTD.

Beg respectfully to announce they have COMMENCED RUNNING A 'BUS, which will meet all Trains. Orders from any part of the Town will have Prompt Attention.

~~~~~~

POSTING IN ALL ITS BRANCHES.

Furniture Removed by Road or Rail.

R. FISHER, Manager.

Waiting outside the Tangier Street premises of the Whitehaven Cab and General Posting Co Ltd is driver Bill Grey with coach and four. The site was later developed as Central Workshops for Cumberland Motor Services and is now a Wetherspoon pub and restaurant. (HPC)

~~~~~~

2. *Whitehaven Motor Service Company Limited.*

Henry Meageen was a cashier in Lord Lonsdale's Colliery office in Whitehaven. He later became Relieving Officer and Registrar for the Borough of Whitehaven and he was also a trustee of Lowther Street Methodist Church. He saw the potential for public transport in the area and arising from this the Whitehaven Motor Service Company Limited was registered on 8th August 1912. In addition to himself and his wife Sarah, other directors were T S Bell an electrical engineer and retailer, George Cowin a toy and glass dealer, and William Clark a provision merchant, all of Whitehaven. The registered office was at 33 King Street.

Messrs Bell and Clark later sold their shares to Henry Meageen thus leaving the company in the hands of the Meageen family and their brother in law George Cowin who continued as a director until his resignation in 1949. The name Meageen became synonymous with buses in West Cumberland for years to come. Henry's son Tom later joined the company becoming Managing Director and Tom's son Harry became Chief Engineer. Harry was a keen motor cyclist and participated in the Isle of Man TT Races.

The company commenced with excursion business using an Arrol-Johnston charabanc XS 102 acquired second-hand from Knott End on Sea and a new Commercial Car charabanc AO 1636. They were named 'Lady Favourite' and 'Lady Florence'. Tom Meageen told the story of how he and his father travelled to Knott End to purchase the Arrol-Johnston. They also hired the driver and at 7pm on a dirty June evening set off on the 100 or so miles journey to Whitehaven. The vehicle had a maximum speed of 12mph and they eventually arrived in Whitehaven at 5am the following morning. Local bus service operation commenced in October 1912 with a service between Whitehaven and Cleator Moor operating on Thursdays and Saturdays. The timetable, as operated from 14th May 1914, for this service is reproduced. The First World War prevented further expansion and the service was suspended in September 1914. At the end of 1914 the registered office was moved from 33 King Street to the premises of the Whitehaven Cab and Posting Company, which the Meageens had purchased and which were situated in Tangier Street , the site of which later became the Central Works for the bus company.

Following the end of the War, expansion took place and by 1920 there were services from Whitehaven to Frizington, via Cleator Moor, to Egremont and to Maryport via Workington.

The Time Table for September 1920 is reproduced. A major event in 1920 was that British Automobile Traction Limited purchased a half share in the company and arising from this, the name was changed, in June 1921, to Cumberland Motor Services Limited.

No. 123665

Certificate of Incorporation.

I Hereby Certify, that the WHITEHAVEN MOTOR SERVICE COMPANY LIMITED is this day Incorporated under the Companies (Consolidation) Act, 1908, and that the Company is **Limited.**

Given under my hand at London this Eighth day of August, One Thousand Nine Hundred and twelve.

Fees and Deed Stamps ... £3. 10s. 0d.

Stamp Duty on Capital ... £3. 15s. 0d.

GEO. J. SARGENT,
Assistant Registrar of Joint Stock Companies.

The original Leyland charabanc TB 1211 'Lady Betty' is shown with N Hamilton, H Davidson and T Conway. (HPC)

Whitehaven Motor Service Co.
LIMITED

The Chara-a-bancs

WILL RUN BETWEEN

CLEATOR MOOR

AND

WHITEHAVEN

COMMENCING

THURSDAY MAY 14th 1914

THURSDAYS		SATURDAYS	
LEAVE WHITEHAVEN	LEAVE CLEATOR MOOR	LEAVE WHITEHAVEN	LEAVE CLEATOR MOOR
9.45	10.45	2.15	3 .0
2. 0	3. 0	4. 0	4.30
3.30	4. 0	5. 0	5.30
4.30	5. 0	6. 0	6.30
6. 0	6.30	7. 0	7.30
9. 0	9.30	8. 0	8.30
		9. 0	9.30
		10. 0	10.30
		11. 0	11.30

FARES TO HENSINGHAM 4d
KEEKLE & CLEATOR MOOR 6d

A busy scene in Eden Street, Silloth showing, nearest the camera, a Vulcan charabanc CW 3253 new in September 1920 and one of two owned by Whitehaven Cab and General Posting Co. Ltd. Both passed to Cumberland Motor Services and were rebodied by Massey Bros. in late 1922. (HPC)

Receiving attention adjacent Bransty Arch is Leyland charabanc 'Lady Margaret' TB 1184 dating from 1920. The Grand Hotel and part of Bransty Station are visible through the arch. Note the children playing around, something which would be impossible with today's traffic conditions. (HPC)

Below: Extract from part of a 1920 timetable. (HPC)

THE WHITEHAVEN MOTOR SERVICE COMPANY LTD

CUMBERLAND

DAILY MOTOR OMNIBUS TIMETABLE From SEPT. 1st 1920

UNTIL FURTHER NOTICE

WHITEHAVEN, DISTINGTON, HARRINGTON, WORKINGTON, FLIMBY, MARYPORT

	A.M	A.M	A.M	P.M	P.M	P.M	P.M	P.M	P.M
WHITEHAVEN	7 30	9 00	11 00	1 00	2 00	4 00	6 00	7 00	8 30
HOWGATE	7 35	9 10	11 10	1 10	2 10	4 10	6 10	7 10	8 40
DISTINGTON	7 45	9 20	11 20	1 20	2 20	4 20	6 20	7 20	8 50
HARRINGTON	8 00	9 30	11 30	1 30	2 00	4 30	6 30	7 30	9 00
WORKINGTON	8 05	9 40	11 40	1 40	2 40	4 40	6 40	7 40	9 10
SIDDICK		9 50	11 50	1 50	2 50	4 50	6 50	7 50	
FLIMBY		10 00	12 00	2 00	3 00	5 00	7 00	8 00	
MARYPORT		10 15	12 15	2 15	3 15	5 15	7 15	8 15	

	A.M	A.M	P.M	P.M	P.M	P.M	P.M	P.M	
MARYPORT		10 30	12 30	2 30	3 30	5 30	7 30	8 30	
FLIMBY		10 40	12 40	2 40	3 40	5 40	7 40	8 40	
SIDDICK		10 50	12 50	2 50	3 50	5 50	7 50	8 50	
WORKINGTON	8 10	11 0	1 00	3 00	4 00	6 00	8 00	9 00	9 15
HARRINGTON	8 20	11 10	1 10	3 10	4 10	6 10	8 10	9 10	9 25
DISTINGTON	8 30	11 20	1 20	3 20	4 20	6 20	8 20	9 20	9 35
HOWGATE	8 40	11 30	1 30	3 30	4 30	6 30	8 30	9 30	9 45
WHITEHAVEN	8 55	11 45	1 45	3 45	4 45	6 45	8 45	9 45	10 00

SUNDAYS

MOTOR BUS WILL
LEAVE WHITEHAVEN
9am 2pm 5 30pm
LEAVE MARYPORT
10 30am 3 30pm
7 30pm

CLEATOR DISTRICT

WHITEHAVEN, KEEKLE, CLEATOR MOOR, WATH BROW, FRIZINGTON

	A.M	A.M	A.M	P.M	P.M	P.M	P.M	P.M	P.M	P.M	P.M	P.M	P.M
WHITEHAVEN	7 45	9 00	11 00	12 00	1 00	2 00	3 00	4 00	5 00	6 00	7 00	8 30	9 00
HENSINGHAM	7 50	9 10	11 10	12.10	1 10	2 10	3 10	4 10	5 10	6 10	7 10	8 40	9 10
KEEKLE	8 0	9 15	11 15	12 15	1 15	2 15	3 15	4 15	5 15	6 15	7 15	8 45	9 15

	A.M	A.M	P.M	P.M	P.M	P.M	P.M	P.M	P.M	P.M	P.M	P.M	P.M
FRIZINGTON	8 25	10 00	12 00	1 00	2 00	3 00	4 00	5 00	6 00	7 00	8 00	9 20	10 00
WATH BROW	8 35	10 10	12 10	1 10	2 10	3 10	4 10	5 10	6 10	7 10	8 10	9 30	10 10
CLEATOR M'R	8 40	10 15	12 15	1 15	2 15	3 15	4 15	5 15	6 15	7 15	8 15	9 35	10 15

3. Cumberland Motor Services Limited.

CUMBERLAND
MOTOR SERVICES,
LIMITED.

TIME TABLE
JULY 4th, 1921,
and Until Further Notice.

Registered Office: Tangier Street, Whitehaven.
T. MEAGEEN, Manager.
'PHONE, 26.

Printed by the "Whitehaven News," Ltd.

The first 'Cumberland' Time Table was produced in 1921 and this included services as follows :-

Whitehaven to Carlisle via Workington, Maryport, Wigton.
Whitehaven to Keswick via Workington, Cockermouth.
Whitehaven to Frizington via Cleator Moor.
Whitehaven to Egremont via Hensingham, Bigrigg.
Carlisle to Silloth via Wigton, Abbeytown.
Maryport to Cockermouth.

Around this time unregulated bus services were developing in many towns and this was causing concern to local authorities, some of whom introduced Bye-Laws in an attempt to control the situation. One such authority was the Borough of Whitehaven which introduced 'Bye Laws with respect to Omnibuses' in 1921. The document was approved by the Council on 13th July 1921 and signed by George Palmer, Mayor, and E B Croasdell, Town Clerk. It was 'allowed' by the Ministry of Health on 15th August 1921 and signed by Charles Knight, an Assistant Secretary. In addition to the inclusion of regulations covering the behaviour of drivers and conductors and indeed passengers, there were regulations covering stopping places.

The twenties was a decade of development both with regard to services and vehicles. Service development during this time is covered in the book 'Cumberland Motor Services 1921 – 1996' and vehicle development is illustrated by the photographs. Great strides were made in vehicle design during this period which included the introduction of pneumatic tyres and fully enclosed double deck bodies. Vehicles at the end of the decade were completely different to those at the beginning of the decade.

Another activity of the twenties was the acquisition of smaller operators including Telford Brothers, Frizington (1920), Star Bus Services Ltd, Workington (1926), Mrs J Wilson, Whitehaven (1927), also Armstrong and Siddle Motor and Transport Company Ltd, Penrith (1928). This was an activity which was to increase in the next decade.

One of the first new vehicles to be delivered to Cumberland Motor Services was No 5, a 1921 Daimler Y type with body by Massey Bros. of Wigan. It was photographed for the body builders before delivery. (RMC)

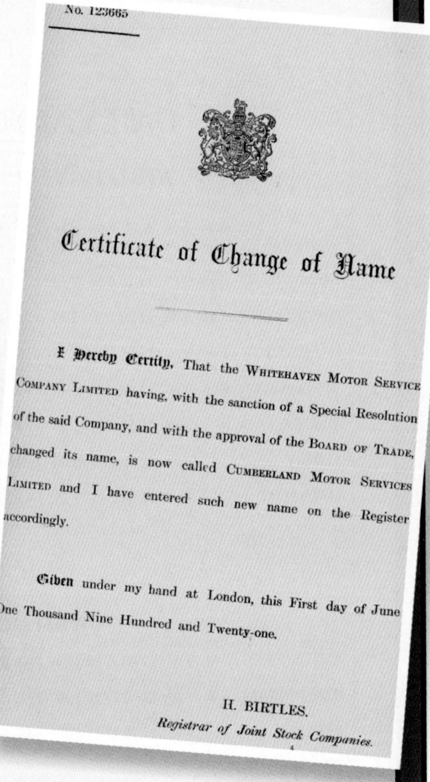

No. 123665

Certificate of Change of Name

I Hereby Certify, That the WHITEHAVEN MOTOR SERVICE COMPANY LIMITED having, with the sanction of a Special Resolution of the said Company, and with the approval of the BOARD OF TRADE, changed its name, is now called CUMBERLAND MOTOR SERVICES LIMITED and I have entered such new name on the Register accordingly.

Given under my hand at London, this First day of June One Thousand Nine Hundred and Twenty-one.

H. BIRTLES.
Registrar of Joint Stock Companies.

This 1921 Daimler Y type AO 6901, fleet No. 25, was fitted with a second-hand double-deck body ex-London General Omnibus Co. It is shown at Bransty Row, Whitehaven with the carriage sheds of Bransty Railway station in the background. (HPC)

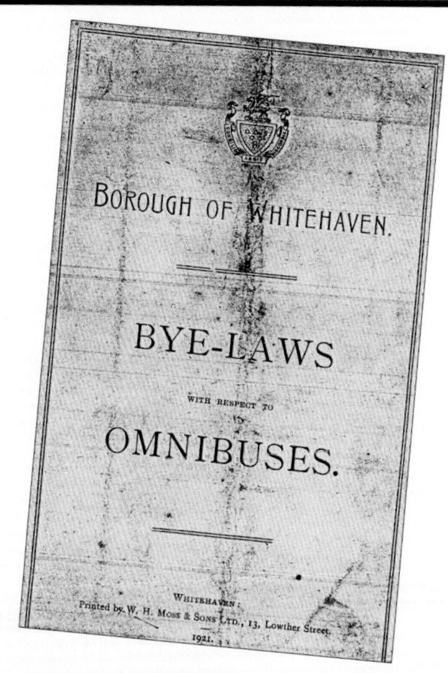

BOROUGH OF WHITEHAVEN.

BYE-LAWS

WITH RESPECT TO

OMNIBUSES.

WHITEHAVEN:
Printed by W. H. Moss & Sons Ltd., 13, Lowther Street.
1921.

Leyland-bodied Leyland SGH7 No. 56 photographed by the builder before delivery in 1924. Note the solid tyres which were later replaced by pneumatics. It was typical of vehicles produced at that time but made obsolete by vehicles delivered a few years later. (LM)

In 1925 ten Daimler Y-type chassis with Massey Bros. bodies were purchased and one of these, No 20, RM 1040 was photographed for the makers when new. (HPC)

Photographed in Aspatria with driver Joe Crellin sitting at the wheel is 1921 Daimler Y-type with Dodson body, *en route* to Carlisle. (HPC)

Workington Bus Station

A notable event in 1926 was the opening of the first purpose-built covered bus station in England, at Murray Road, Workington. This photograph is thought to have been taken shortly after the opening, possibly to mark the event. (SCC)

The first vehicles in the fleet with pneumatic tyres were two AEC 411 models with Massey Bros. bodies. They were numbered 66 and 67, RM 1991 and RM 2049, being new in 1925. (CMS)

OFFICIAL
Bus Time Table.
JUNE 8th, 1926,
Until Further Notice.
MOTOR
CUMBERLAND
SERVICES
Ltd
Price ONE PENNY.
Cumberland Motor Services Ltd.
T. MEAGEEN, Manager.
Registered Office:
TANGIER STREET, WHITEHAVEN.
PHONE 28.

Westmorland Motor Services was established by the Meageens in 1925 to operate a service from Keswick to Kendal. Number 15, RM 1520, was one of five AEC 411 models with Massey Bros. bodies, purchased for this purpose. (CMS)

Lions and Tigers

The Leyland Lion became one of the most popular and respected single-deck buses of the late 'twenties. Cumberland purchased five with Leyland bodies in 1926 and one of these, No. 68, RM 2227 is shown photographed when new by one of Leyland's photographers. (LM)

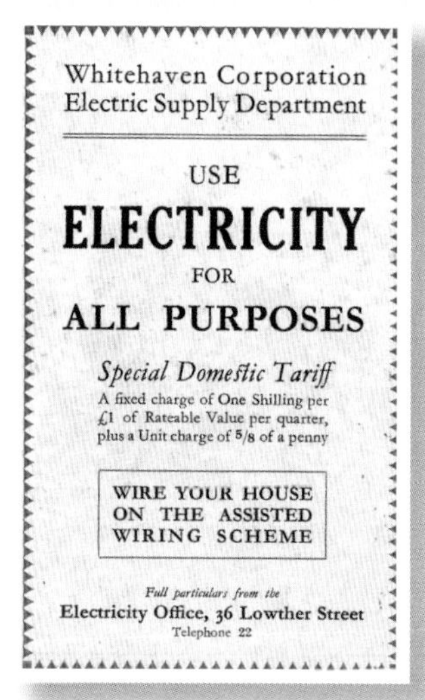

This prewar view looking west along Lowther Street, Whitehaven shows a 1927 Leyland Lion with Massey Bros. body, thought to be No. 3, RM 4107, passing the entrance to Castle Park *en route* to Hensingham Square.

After the Lion, Leyland introduced a heavier duty model and gave it the name 'Tiger'. Number 31 was one of four TS2 models with Massey Bros. bodies purchased in 1930. All were rebodied by Massey Bros. in 1939 as illustrated later, either as coaches or with coach style bodies provided with bus seats. (HPC)

In 1930 a further four Tiger TS2 models, also with Massey Bros. bodies were received and numbered 111-114. All were rebodied by Myers and Bowman of Distington in 1938. A photograph of No. 111 after rebodying is shown on page 70. (HPC)

Early Double-Deckers

DOUGLAS I.O.M. and
DUBLIN via SILLOTH
(In connection with L. & N.E.R.)
Sailings from **SILLOTH** every Tuesday & Saturday
Through fares and rates from various parts of North of England and South of Scotland.

Silloth to Douglas { 13/- Cabin return
9/- Steerage ,,
Valid 1 Month

For Full Particulars Apply:
The Station Master, L. & N.E. Rly., Silloth
Telephone: SILLOTH 17
Telegrams: "STATIONMASTER, SILLOTH."
and at L. & N.E. Rly. Stations

Dublin & Silloth Steamship Co. Ltd.
Palgrave Murphy Ltd., (Managers)
17 EDEN QUAY, DUBLIN

The company's first new double-decker was a Guy FCX model purchased in 1927 but it was not successful and the company turned to Leyland Motors for the next double-deckers. Six lowbridge open staircase TD1 models were purchased in 1929 and one of these was photographed (*above*) when new by Leyland Motors. The Titans obviously gave a good account of themselves and further examples were purchased in 1930 and 1931 but these had enclosed staircases. One of the 1931 models, No. 18, was photographed (*right*) by the makers in Carlisle just after starting its return journey to Whitehaven. (LM both)

A scene in Whitehaven's Tangier Street, thought to have been taken in the early 'thirties , shows *The Grand Hotel* together with the entrance/exit to the bus station and also the Central Engineering Works on the right. The rear view of the double-decker clearly shows the enclosed rear and it is thought to be one of the 1931 deliveries. The telephone kiosk at the extreme right was a familiar landmark for many years. (WM)

BIG VALUE

LARGEST SELECTIONS
NEWEST GOODS

IN

Ladies', Gent's and Children's Wear

House Furniture, &c.

AT

FRANK FOWLES LTD.

THE SQUARE
CLEATOR MOOR

... PHONE 63

A photograph of Cleator Moor Square taken in the early 'thirties shows two Leyland TD1 double- deckers heading towards Wath Brow and a Leyland Lion making for Whitehaven. The building on the extreme right housed Frank Fowles store, a business that advertised regularly in Cumberland timetables and other literature. (WM)

AEC was very keen to sell vehicles to Cumberland and two Regent models were on hire and subsequently purchased by Cumberland. The picture, left, shows No. 12 with Short Bros. body in Duke Street, Whitehaven at what was the Duke Street Bus Stop for many years when vehicles from the bus station travelled along Tangier Street and then turned left into Duke Street. It was purchased in 1931.

This photograph shows No. 47, with Massey body, at the head of a long line of Leyland vehicles on what appears to be a major private hire job. This vehicle was purchased in 1932. (HPC)

Single-Deckers of the 'Thirties

AEC was more successful with single-deck sales to CMS and provided nine Regal models with Harrington bodies in 1932. Six, equipped as coaches, are seen later. Three were buses, one of which – No. 9 – is shown above in Carlisle. (RMC)

Leyland continued the use of the type name 'Lion' for the LT5A model produced in the mid-'thirties. Cumberland took five examples with Massey Bros. bodies in 1934 and one of these, No. 38, is shown at Keswick. (CWR)

AEC was again successful in 1936, supplying five single-deck Regal chassis. These were fitted with bodies by H V Burlingham of Blackpool as seen left. Although classified as buses, they were fitted with very comfortable seating and in later years would have been classified as 'dual-purpose'. Number 121 is shown at Carlisle bus station. (CWR)

The final single-deck service buses supplied in the 'thirties comprised five Leyland TS8 models with bodies by Massey Bros. They also had particularly comfortable seating and could have been classified as 'dual-purpose'. Number 139 was photographed by Massey Bros. when new. (STA)

Double-Deckers of the mid-'Thirties

By now the diesel engine had gained predominance over the petrol engine and all double-deckers supplied new to Cumberland from 1936 were fitted as new with diesel engines. Also body builders were moving away from box like structures and attempting to apply some shape, leading to the appearance of sloping or curved fronts and rears. Reference was made earlier to the two AEC Regents 12 and 47. They were both replaced by two identical AEC Regents in 1936 fitted with Massey Bros. bodies. Number 47 is shown above left at Carlisle bus station awaiting departure to Whitehaven. Also purchased in 1936 were nine Leyland TD4 models and they carried bodies by Massey Bros. identical to those fitted to the two AEC Regents. Number 118 waits in Keswick bus station, above right, for departure to Whitehaven. (JFH; OS)

No double-deck vehicles were purchased in 1937, but in 1938 Leyland supplied five TD5 models and these carried bodies by Massey Bros. to the same design as that for the 1936 vehicles. They were numbered 133-7 and No. 135 was photographed at Leyland's South Works by one of their photographers when new. (STA)

After the war the 1936 and 1938 double-deckers were either rebuilt or rebodied. One of those rebodied was BRM 596 originally numbered 132 but renumbered 291 after being rebodied by Eastern Coach Works in 1949. After withdrawal it passed to Barton Transport for further service and was later bought for preservation. It is shown in Whitehaven bus station when attending the Open Day and Rally at Lillyhall in May 1996.

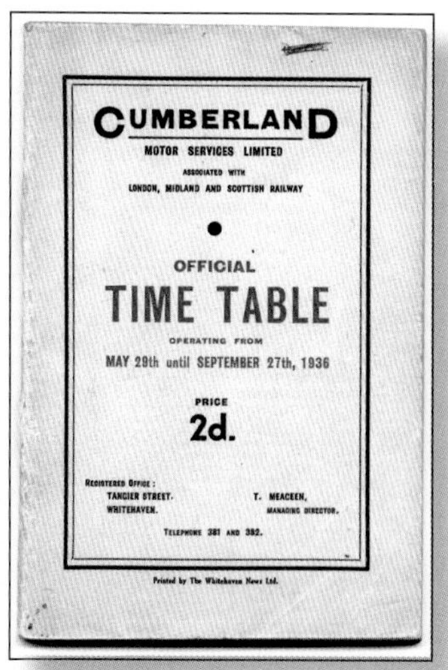

CUMBERLAND

MOTOR SERVICES LIMITED

ASSOCIATED WITH

LONDON, MIDLAND AND SCOTTISH RAILWAY

OFFICIAL

TIME TABLE

OPERATING FROM

MAY 29th until SEPTEMBER 27th, 1936

PRICE

2d.

REGISTERED OFFICE:
TANGIER STREET.
WHITEHAVEN.

T. MEACEEN,
MANAGING DIRECTOR.

TELEPHONE 381 AND 382.

Printed by The Whitehaven News Ltd.

Coaching in the 'Thirties

Three of the six Harrington-bodied AEC Regal coaches supplied in 1936 are illustrated in this posed view with their smartly turned out drivers. Note the white coats and white topped caps used in summer. (HPC)

Number 55, left, was a Burlingham-bodied Leyland TS7 coach, one of three supplied in 1936. (OS)

As previously mentioned, 1932 Leyland TS2 No. 31, seen lower left and below, was rebodied in 1939 with this luxury coach body by Massey Bros. and fitted with the longer 'Cov Rad' radiator conversion at the same time. This was an attempt to modernise the appearance of the by then very dated chassis front. An indication of the high standard of interior finish is shown in the view below, note the deep leather-trimmed moquette seats. (STA)

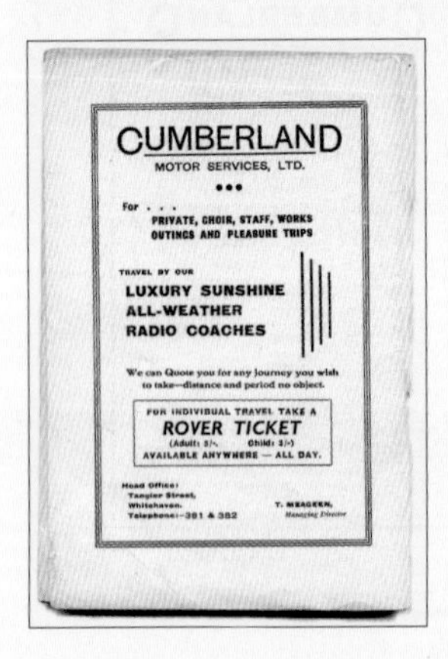

CUMBERLAND
MOTOR SERVICES, LTD.

For . . .
PRIVATE, CHOIR, STAFF, WORKS OUTINGS AND PLEASURE TRIPS

TRAVEL BY OUR
LUXURY SUNSHINE
ALL-WEATHER
RADIO COACHES

We can Quote you for any journey you wish to take—distance and period no object.

FOR INDIVIDUAL TRAVEL TAKE A
ROVER TICKET
(Adult: 5/-. Child: 3/-)
AVAILABLE ANYWHERE — ALL DAY.

Head Office:
Tangier Street,
Whitehaven.
Telephone:—381 & 382

T. MEAGEEN,
Managing Director

GR VI 1937

Coronation Year Tours

by Cumberland Motor Services Ltd.
Tangier Street
Whitehaven

No. 1

5 DAYS' SCOTTISH TOUR

to

Aberdeen and the Royal Road

Leaving - FRIDAY, 18th JUNE
Returning TUESDAY, 22nd JUNE

Fare: $5\frac{1}{2}$ Guineas

ITINERARY:

1st DAY—FRIDAY, 18th JUNE.
Leave Whitehaven at 8-30 a.m. for Workington, Maryport, Wigton, Carlisle, Gretna Green, Ecclefechan, Lockerbie, Beattock, Abington, Lanark, Airdrie, Denny, Stirling, and to **Bridge of Allan.** (Overnight stay).

2nd DAY—SATURDAY, 19th JUNE.
Leave Bridge of Allan at 9 a.m. for Dunblane and Perth, Coupar Angus and Glamis Castle to Forfar. Thence to Brechin and Montrose and coast road to Bervie, Stonehaven and **Aberdeen.** (Overnight stay).

3rd DAY—SUNDAY, 20th JUNE.
Leave Aberdeen at 9 a.m. for the Royal Road *via* Banchory, Aboyne, Ballater, Balmoral Castle; thence by Devil's Elbow and the famous Spittal of Glenshee to Blairgowrie and to **Perth.** (Overnight stay).

4th DAY—MONDAY, 21st JUNE.
Leave Perth at 10 a.m. for Methven, Crieff, Gleneagles, Dunblane, Stirling, Falkirk, Linlithgow, **Edinburgh.** (Stay overnight)

5th AND LAST DAY—TUESDAY, 22nd JUNE.
Morning in Edinburgh free for individual action. After lunch leave Edinburgh for Galashiels, Selkirk, Hawick, Mosspaul, Langholm, Canonbie, Longtown, Carlisle, Wigton, Maryport, Workington and Whitehaven.

Fare includes FIRST-CLASS HOTEL ACCOMMODATION comprising Dinner, Bed, Breakfast and Gratuities each day commencing with late Dinner on the first day and terminating with Breakfast on the last day.

No. 3

10 Days' Sunny South Tour

DEVON

and the

CORNISH RIVIERA

Leaving WEDNESDAY, 4th AUGUST
Returning - FRIDAY, 13th AUGUST

Fare: 11 Guineas

ITINERARY:

1st DAY—WEDNESDAY, 4th AUGUST.
By Six Lakes Route *via* Bassenthwaite Lake, Derwentwater, Thirlmere, Grasmere, Rydal Water, Windermere to Kendal, Lancaster, Preston, Wigan, Warrington to **CHESTER.** (Overnight stay at Chester).

2nd DAY—THURSDAY, 5th AUGUST.
From Chester to Whitchurch, Wem, Shrewsbury, Church Stretton, Craven Arms, Ludlow, Leominster, Hereford, Ross-on-Wye, Gloucester to **BRISTOL.** (Overnight stay at Bristol).

3rd DAY—FRIDAY, 6th AUGUST.
From Bristol to Axbridge, Cheddar Gorge, Wells, Glastonbury, Bridgwater, Dunster, Blackmoor Gate, Minehead, Porlock, Lynmouth, Lynton, Combe Martin to **ILFRACOMBE.** (Overnight stay at Ilfracombe).

4th DAY—SATURDAY, 7th AUGUST.
From Ilfracombe for Barnstaple, Bideford, Bude, Camelford, Wade Bridge, Newquay, Perranporth, Redruth, Camborne, Hayle to **PENZANCE.** (Overnight stay at Penzance).

The Outbreak of War

With the outbreak of war in September 1939 the effect on services was almost immediate, with restriction on the supply of fuel. Wartime timetables were introduced and comprised folded sheets, one covering the northern area and the other the southern area. The first was issued on 7th October 1939 and these were regularly updated as the fuel situation worsened or eased. Earlier in the year four Leyland Titan TD5 double-deckers had been received.

CUMBERLAND
MOTOR SERVICES LIMITED

TIME TABLE

SOUTHERN SECTION

Operating from
Saturday, October 7th, 1939
Until Further Notice

PRICE 1d.

T. MEAGEEN,
Managing Director.
Registered Office:
Tangier Street, Whitehaven.
Telephone 381 and 382.

Two of the four new vehicles Nos. 145 and 146, had bodies by East Lancashire Coachbuilders, a company which had been re-formed in 1938 as covered in the author's book *East Lancashire Coachbuilders* published by Venture Publications. One of this pair is shown photographed for the coachbuilder when new. (HPC)

The other two, Nos. 143 and 144, had bodies by regular supplier, Massey Bros., but had a more curved front and rear compared to previous bodies from this builder. Number 144 was photographed for the coachbuilder when new at the Pemberton works. (STA)

In 1954 No. 144 was fitted with the 1948 Burlingham body removed from Leyland TD2 No. 152 when the chassis was scrapped. It is shown with another item of Whitehaven history in the background, the Whitehaven Bransty railway station building. (RCD)

Second-Hand Vehicles

West Cumberland was declared a 'safe area' during the war and received many evacuees. There were also factories built for the war effort, so that these factors combined to present a requirement for additional buses, and a number of used vehicles were purchased to meet this demand.

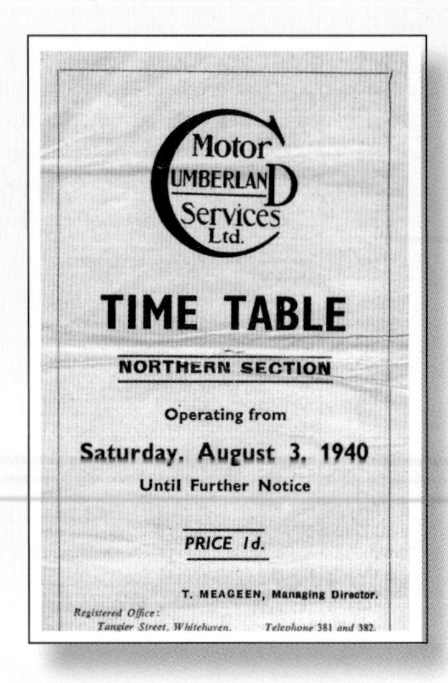

Motor
CUMBERLAND
Services
Ltd.

TIME TABLE

NORTHERN SECTION

Operating from

Saturday, August 3, 1940

Until Further Notice

PRICE 1d.

T. MEAGEEN, Managing Director.

Registered Office:
Tangier Street, Whitehaven. *Telephone 381 and 382.*

This photograph taken in New Road Garage, Whitehaven, shows No. 86, one of six Leyland TD1 double-deckers which were purchased from Southdown Motor Services along with three TD2 double-deckers. The TD2 double-deckers numbered 96, 99 and 100 were fitted with Gardner diesel engines and used particularly on Whitehaven Town Services. The other two vehicles seen here, numbered 154 and 156, were ex-London Transport Leyland TD2 models with open staircase bodies. They were rebodied in 1943 as illustrated on page 18. (SLP)

In addition to the two open staircase models there were five with closed staircase bodies also ex-London Transport, similar to No. 157 shown here loading at Whitehaven bus station for Hensingham Square. All five were fitted with Gardner diesel engines and became regular performers on Whitehaven Town Services. Note the half door to the driver's cab. There was a roll-up blind with a Perspex window but these were rarely used as it seems that the Perspex window became opaque and thus seriously restricted vision. (SLP)

After the war all five of the ex-London Transport vehicles, together with the three ex-Southdown TD2s, received new highbridge bodies by HV Burlingham of Blackpool, as illustrated here by No. 157. All returned to work on Whitehaven Town Services. (RM)

More New Vehicles

In May 1940 the Board agreed to purchase ten Leyland TD7 double-deck chassis at a cost of £962 9s 0d each and to order five Massey bodies at £790 each and five East Lancashire bodies at £795 each. The total cost for ten double-deckers was therefore £17,549! They were delivered in 1941 and were entirely to peace time specification.

One of the Massey-bodied vehicles was No. 160, shown here in Carlisle bus station about to depart for Cockermouth. By this time it had been painted in the wartime livery of grey with white relief. (SLP)

Photographed at Whitehaven in the postwar period and seen below is one of the East Lancashire-bodied examples, No. 164. (RCD)

A further four Leyland TD7 double-deckers arrived during 1941. Clearly they had been built to a different specification, as seen below centre left and right. In fact they had been bodied by Park Royal for Southdown Motor Services who, because of the outbreak of war, did not need them. Cumberland purchased them from Southdown and had them repainted into Cumberland livery at Massey Bros. , Wigan, at a cost of £47 10s 0d per vehicle. These photographs were taken at Wigan before the journey to Whitehaven. They were re-registered EAO 724-7 before entering service. (STA)

In 1950 all of the Park Royal-bodied examples, together with two of the Massey-bodied vehicles and two of the East Lancashire-bodied ones, were rebodied by H V Burlingham in Blackpool, and renumbered 295-302, thus taking Cumberland fleet numbers over 300 for the first time. Here, the first of the batch, number 295, is seen and the front upper-deck side windows will be seen to have echoes of the Ribble White Lady coach-seated double-deckers of the time. (RCD)

The Utilities

The first utility double-deck bus chassis were manufactured by Guy Motors Ltd who produced a rugged chassis fitted with either a 5LW or 6LW Gardner engine. Bodies were built by several coachbuilders to a standard specification.

Cumberland's first utility double-deckers were five Guy Arab I models with Gardner 6LW engines and bodies by Brush to the standard utility specification. Number 185 is shown above left when new at Carlisle bus station. Three Daimler CWG5 models with similar bodies and numbered 186-8 were also purchased. The next utilities were Guy Arab II models with bodies by Northern Counties Motor & Engineering Co. Ltd of Wigan. This firm had been given special dispensation to continue using metal framed components from stock rather than timber framing of the standard specification. They were numbered 202-15 and Nos. 205-15 had slatted wooden seats. Number 207 is seen above right in Cockermouth Main Street. (LMu; SLP)

A number of existing chassis were reconditioned and rebodied by Northern Coachbuilders of Newcastle upon Tyne, to the same standard specification as bodies for new vehicles. The above photograph shows No. 156, one of the ex-London Transport Leyland TD2s, which previously carried open staircase bodies, at Whitehaven bus station after rebodying. It is ironical that these buses probably had the most substantial and most comfortable seating of all wartime bodies but because they were on reconditioned chassis, were used mainly on Town Services and other short distance routes. (SLP)

The only new single-deckers available during wartime were Bedford OWB models, most of the bodies on these being by Duple. Cumberland were allocated two of these in October 1942 at a cost of £740 each! A further 13 followed in 1944 and 1945. They had slatted wooden seats but when the above photograph of No. 72, dating from 1944, was taken in Workington depot in the postwar period, replacement upholstered seats had been provided. (RM)

On 21st January 1940, with snow on the ground, Whitehaven's Grand Hotel was destroyed by fire. On 6th June 1940 the Cumberland Board agreed to purchase the site for £3,035 and a 'temporary' garage was erected on the site and remained there until 1991! Some things are better for not being hurried. (HPC)

Postwar Fleet Renewal

The first new vehicles to arrive in the fleet after the war were five Leyland PS1 single-deckers bodied by Massey Bros. This photograph at Keswick bus station illustrates the effect of later rebuilding with rubber mounted glazing. (RCD)

A further four Leyland PS1 single-deckers arrived and these had bodies by Associated Coachbuilders. There should have been five but one was diverted to H & I Moffett of Cleator Moor in exchange for a coach, also with ACB body which became No. 180 in the Cumberland fleet. The photograph shows No. 124 at Whitehaven. (RM)

Six Duple-bodied Bedford coaches were purchased and arrived during 1947/8 numbered 248-53. Number 251 is shown at Keswick bus station. (CWR)

The first postwar luxury coaches, apart from No 180 previously mentioned, were ten Leyland PS1 models with bodies by Associated Coachbuilders. Shown standing where property had been destroyed in the blitz during WW2 at Piccadilly, Manchester is No. 26. Weekend troop specials for military personnel on 48-hour passes regularly used this area. (AEJ)

The other single-deckers in the immediate postwar period were ten Leyland PS1 models with Burlingham bodies, some of which were later retrofitted with coach seating and improved interior trim at a time when there was a shortage of coaches. Shown at Carlisle bus station in the view above left, alongside an ACB-bodied coach, is No. 196 (JDE)

The ten ACB-bodied coaches were followed by ten with bodies by H V Burlingham. One of these, No.199, was photographed at Piccadilly, Manchester and is seen above alongside one of the later Leyland Royal Tiger coaches. (AEJ)

By the time the next new coaches arrived in 1953, the underfloor- engined chassis had become the norm for single-deckers. Three coaches on Leyland Royal Tiger chassis, and with Leyland bodies, were numbered 345-7 and No. 346 was photographed by Leyland Motors when new. (LM)

Postwar Double-Deckers

A total of thirty Leyland PD1 double-deckers arrived in the period 1948/9, ten having bodies by Massey Bros. as illustrated here by No. 247 at the Whitehaven Grand Hotel site. Numerically, it was the last Massey-bodied vehicle to be received by Cumberland, thus ending an association going back to 1922. (RM)

The other 20 double-deckers had bodies by Northern Coachbuilders as shown above by No. 231 photographed in Workington bus station. It was operating on Town Service 48 to Harrington which was, at that time, the most frequent service in the timetable, operating every 7½ minutes. Also visible is the rear of Eastern Coach Works-bodied Leyland Royal Tiger No. 325. (RM)

The PD1s were quickly followed in 1949 by 22 PD2/1s with Leyland metal-framed bodies. There should have been 30, but the last eight were diverted to Crosville on completion, complete with Cumberland registration numbers. Seen at Carlisle bus station, just arrived from Whitehaven, is No. 282 the last of the batch. Note the conductor with his Willebrew ticket machine. (HPC)

Parked at Maryport bus station is Northern Counties-bodied Guy Arab II No. 214 which had been rebuilt with postwar style destination equipment. At the same time it would have had its slatted wooden seats replaced by upholstered seats removed from buses which were being rebodied. (CMS)

A scene on the Grand Hotel site in Whitehaven in the early 'fifties shows Massey-bodied Leyland TD7 No. 159 facing the camera, a partial side view of one of the East Lancashire-bodied Leyland TD7s flanked on both sides by vehicles with Northern Coachbuilders utility bodies. Behind No. 159 is a Northern Coachbuilders-bodied Leyland PD1. (HPC)

The Last New Leylands – for Several Years

KRM 261 was one of 20 Leyland PD2/12 models with Leyland bodies delivered in 1951 and numbered 303-22. In the 1961 renumbering scheme it became No. 379. It is shown at the Grand Hotel site in Whitehaven. A further ten similar vehicles were delivered in 1952 and numbered 328-37. (GL)

The first underfloor-engined single-deckers to enter the fleet were five Leyland Royal Tigers with bodies by Eastern Coach Works of Lowestoft and numbered 323-7. This view, right, shows LAO 148 in Cockermouth Main Street after it had become 154 in the 1961 renumbering scheme. (AD)

The next single-deckers were also Royal Tigers but with Leyland bodies to this rather box-like design shown by MAO 108, below, at Keswick bus station. It was originally No. 340 and was renumbered 157 in 1961. These bodies were rebuilt by Cumberland and in the process lost their cream centre bands and had the window surrounds painted cream. The ECW bodies on the earlier Royal Tigers did not seem to need such extensive rebuilding. (RCD)

In order to expedite Cumberland's commitment to Leyland arising from the large advance order previously placed, the Tilling Group ordered five Royal Tigers with Eastern Coach Works bodies but allocated them to United Automobile Services. All five came to Cumberland from United in 1967 and were numbered 162-6. Shown leaving Workington bus station annexe, below, is No. 166. (PN)

GREYSOUTHERN
MARYPORT
EWANRIGG

The Bristol Era

Despite being part of the Tilling Group since 1942 the company had remained faithful to Leyland as vehicle supplier rather than the Bristol/Eastern Coach Works combination which was the norm for the Tilling Group. The reason was the majority shareholding held by the Meageens and in 1947 Tom Meageen placed a large advance order with Leyland covering vehicle requirements up to the mid-'fifties. The reason given for this was the extended delivery times for vehicles in the postwar period. Eventually this commitment to Leyland was discharged and the Company then followed Tilling practice in ordering Bristols. The first Bristols were coaches and these were quickly followed by double-deckers which were of the recently introduced 'Lodekka' design. This was revolutionary in that a low floor design enabled a body of conventional layout to be employed within the confines of a low height double decker 13ft 5ins high without resorting to the awkward sunken gangway alongside seats for four in the upper saloon.

One of the first batch of Bristol 'Lodekkas' was ORM 135 shown above at Wigton after renumbering to No. 400 in 1961. When supplied they were numbered 353 -7 and were the last double-deckers supplied with the traditional Cumberland postwar destination equipment layout. They had higher backed seats which made them very comfortable for longer journeys. (GL)

The next batch of 'Lodekkas' had 'T' type destination displays and conventional bus seats. Number 411, formerly numbered 364, is shown at Whitehaven bus station. (HPC)

When delivered, the first Bristol coaches were in a cream livery with black trim. They were later repainted in Tilling red and cream as illustrated by No. 279, ORM 134, one of the second batch of such coaches to be delivered. When new it was numbered 352. (RCD)

Bristol buses soon became a familiar sight on the roads of Cumberland. Photographed at Wigton bus station is VAO 386, dating from 1958, originally numbered 386 and renumbered 428 in 1961. (PN)

In 1957/8 eight Lodekkas were purchased specifically for Town Service operation in Whitehaven and Workington. They had four-speed gearboxes and were without platform doors. They were later given 'T' prefixes to the fleet numbers to distinguish them from other Lodekkas which were given 'C' prefixes. In 1959 a further five similar vehicles were purchased. Three of these, Nos. 387-9 had Bristol rather than Gardner engines. One of these, formerly 388 but later renumbered 430, is shown at Whitehaven bus station. The author recalls asking the late Algie Corlett, former Works Superintendent, what he thought of the Bristol engines. His response was immediate and positive. 'Next best thing to a Gardner; with dry liners they would have been as good'. Praise indeed from a Gardner engine enthusiast. (PN)

The standard Bristol single-deck service bus of the time was the MW, an example of which is shown here on the parking ground at Whitehaven with another piece of Whitehaven history in the background, the Quaker Oats building which has long since disappeared from the scene. (GL)

An example of the MW with coach body similar in outline to the earlier LS type is shown below at Lakeside, Windermere with the motor vessel 'Swan' in the background after its refurbishment in 1964. Originally numbered 392 when new in 1959, XAO 600 became 284 in the 1961 scheme. (CMS)

Rebodied and Rebuilt

The quality of timber available for coachbuilding in the period after World War II was poor, being largely unseasoned, and resulted in many bodies requiring rebuilding or replacing prematurely.

The eleven ACB-bodied Leyland PS1 coaches were all rebodied in the late 'fifties or 1960. Ten received new bodies which were built in the body shop at Whitehaven under the expert attention of the late John Twentyman, the body shop foreman. The author recalls asking John when writing the first book, if there were any drawings of these bodies still available, to which he replied 'We didn't have drawings, we just built them!' This photograph of No. 113, previously No 34, at Keswick shows the excellent finished result. (AD)

The eleventh vehicle, No. 114, previously No 35, was rebodied by Eastern Coach Works and is shown here at Keswick bus station. (AD)

All the Leyland PD1 double-deckers were rebuilt in the late 'fifties or early 'sixties, a process which involved rubber mounted perimeter glazing, together with changes to the interior trim. Illustrated here is PD1 GAO 766 bodied by Northern Coachbuilders and photographed at Millom. When new it carried fleet No. 228, becoming No. 315 in 1961. (GL)

This photograph, taken in Workington depot in the early 'sixties, indicates that, despite the arrival of the Bristols, there was still a variety of Leylands in the fleet. The photograph shows, left to right, an unidentified Leyland PS1 with Cumberland body, Leyland-bodied Royal Tiger No. 158, Burlingham-bodied Leyland PS1 No. 106, a Leyland-bodied Leyland PD2/1 and a former United Counties ECW-bodied PD1 No. 306. (GL)

The Bristol SC was a lightweight single-deck vehicle introduced in the late 'fifties and intended for rural areas where traffic was light. It was regarded as a rather crude noisy vehicle and in the Cumberland fleet they became known as 'The Sputniks'. It is alleged that the first driver to take one out stated on his return, 'They should have sent that up in the sputnik!' The name stuck. Number 203, previously 402, was photographed at Keswick bus station. Crude they may have been, but operators in flat areas were getting over 20 miles to the gallon out of them. (AD)

In an attractive rural setting in the south of the county, No. 206 makes its way south towards Millom, having connected at Seascale with the vehicle operating the northern leg of service 13 from Whitehaven to Seascale. It was one of three similar vehicles acquired from United Counties in 1963. (GL)

Forward Entrance and Longer Double-Deckers

Ten forward-entrance double-deckers entered the fleet in 1960. Five were Bristol FSF as illustrated by 502 BRM and a similar vehicle parked behind at the Grand Hotel site in Whitehaven. The other five were the longer FLF type and subsequently all forward-entrance double-deckers were of this length. (GL)

The FLF double-deckers were used on a wide variety of services including Town Services and the longer distance services. Number 533 photographed here at Carlisle bus station was new in 1966 as part of a batch of three which were the last such vehicles to enter the fleet. (AD)

Photographed at Whitehaven are FLFs 523 and 522 which were part of a batch numbered 521-4 delivered in March 1964. By this time, Bristol had ceased manufacture of its own engine and offered the Leyland O.600 engine as an alternative to the Gardner and Nos. 522-4 had Leyland engines. Comparative tests were carried out by the engineers between 521 with Gardner 6LX engine and the Leyland-engined examples on Whitehaven Town Services. After 100,000 miles the Gardner engine was still going strong but the Leyland engines were ready for major attention. No further Leyland-engined FLFs were purchased and No. 522 had its Leyland engine replaced by a Gardner 6LX engine in March 1976. (GL)

Despite turning to forward-entrance longer double-deckers, the company still saw a use for traditional rear entrance double-deckers of 27ft length and purchased five registered 109-13 DRM in 1961. The first of these, is shown at Wigton bus station after being renumbered 550. For some time whilst in service it carried an advertisement on the nearside between decks area for the first Cumberland book produced by the Author, in 1983. This vehicle is now preserved in full running order by the 550 Group. (RCD)

Rear-Engined Single-Deckers

The Bristol RE was the first rear-engined single-decker to appear on the market and was generally regarded as the most reliable. Cumberland purchased two in 1966, numbered 250/1. They had Gardner engines and No. 250 had a short life with the company, being withdrawn in 1970 after an accident at Thornhill. Photographed at Cockermouth Main Street, whilst operating the service from Maryport is No. 251. (PN)

The next Bristol REs, with revised body styling incorporating flat fronts, arrived in 1967 and were numbered 252-263. They had Leyland engines. Number 259 was photographed in Tangier Street, Whitehaven, having just left the bus station. (GL)

The REs were versatile vehicles employed on most types of service from Town Services to longer distances. Awaiting departure from Carlisle bus station to Silloth is No. 266 which was one of a batch of 13 numbered 264-76, purchased in 1969. They had Leyland engines and when the engineers complained about this, they were told that by accepting Leyland engines, they were able to purchase the baker's dozen for the price of twelve with Gardner engines. (RCD)

The National Bus Company

The National Bus Company was formed to take over the subsidiary companies which had previously been in the Tilling Group and the British Electric Traction Group. It took effect from 1st January 1969. Initially there was little outward evidence of this as new vehicles were delivered in line with orders previously placed and services continued very much as before. Changes were to come, but these took time to develop.

In 1969 further Bristol REs were delivered, numbered 277-88, but these had deeper windscreens than the previous REs as illustrated by No. 280, above, at Carlisle bus station on service 30 to Whitehaven. (PN)

The Bristol LH was a lightweight single-decker – the LH indicating lightweight horizontal engine. Cumberland took delivery of 17 of these in 1970, numbered 100-16 and No. 115 is shown at St. Bees on the service from Whitehaven which, in those days, was numbered 08. (GL)

Photographed at Carlisle bus station is No 299, one of the final batch of Bristol REs delivered in 1972. Three of the batch, Nos. 296-8, had coach seating and were classed as dual-purpose. These and the REs delivered in 1971 had the double curvature windscreen, rather than the flat screens fitted to earlier examples. The 1971 and the 1972 Bristol REs had the larger Leyland O.680 engine. (AD)

The Leyland National

Leyland, in conjunction with the National Bus Company, developed a new integral single-deck bus which was intended to meet the requirements of the National Bus Company subsidiaries and also to be attractive to municipal and private operators together with the export market. A purpose-designed factory was built at Lillyhall in West Cumberland, for the production of the vehicles. Leyland developed the fixed-head 500 series engine for the vehicle which turned out to be noisy, dirty and thirsty with the result that it was very unpopular with operators. The clatter of the Leyland National became a well recognised sound in the 'seventies. In addition the internal finish to the body was regarded as rather spartan and soon became shabby. The first production Leyland National, ERM 35K was allocated to Cumberland Motor Services and carried fleet number 350.

ERM 35K was delivered in Cumberland's red livery without cream relief and, as indicated in this view at Whitehaven's parking area, was of the dual-doorway pattern. It was subsequently modified to single-door configuration. (AD)

An early view of No. 350 climbing Bransty Brow, Whitehaven, with the bus station in the background and operating the northern part of Town Service 05 on which the vehicle regularly operated when first delivered. (HPC)

Seen on Lowther Street, Whitehaven, passing the Civic Hall in July 1983 is No. 356, one of twelve delivered in 1973.

Bristol FLF No 511, parked at the Haig Colliery terminus of Town Service 01 in Whitehaven, displays the traditional Cumberland red and cream livery with black lining out and wings. The colliery is now closed but is the site of an excellent mining museum complete with winding engine. In earlier years the terminus was known by the rather quaint name of 'Basket House'. (GL)

The Government appointed Mr Frederick (later to become Sir Frederick) Wood as chairman of the National Bus Company. He came from the chemical industry with no previous experience of passenger transport operation. He knew nothing of local operator pride in the appearance of their vehicles and their liveries but was obsessed with 'corporate image' and brought in an industrial designer to assist with this. Standard liveries were introduced across the board. Long distance coaches were to be white with large **NATIONAL** names in red and blue. Service buses were to be either leaf green or an insipid shade of red known as poppy red, with single white band. Local coaches and dual-purpose vehicles were to be half and half fleet colour and white. Fleet names were to be in bland block lettering with a double *N* symbol alongside. Compared to the traditional Cumberland livery, and those of most other operators, this colour scheme looked cheap and nasty and did nothing to engender pride in the various companies involved.

Standing in Main Street Cockermouth, above, having arrived from Maryport is Bristol RE No. 279, displaying the NBC livery.

Contrasting with No. 511, top, and showing the bland NBC livery is Bristol FS No. 557 (*above right*) photographed in Maryport *en route* from Carlisle to Whitehaven. (HPC)

Photographed in Keswick bus station on 27th May 1980 are Bristol MW No. 231 and Bristol RE No. 300, both displaying the NBC livery.

The Workington plant where the Nationals were built was highly automated and the paint line was no exception. One colour, all-over, was the routine, white, poppy red or leaf green. In the early days not even the PTEs could get round this, except by having their vehicles subsequently painted elsewhere. Thus all Cumberland's Leyland Nationals were delivered in a single colour without white band and No. 352 displays this as it crosses from Strand Street to Tangier Street, Whitehaven whilst operating on Town Service 09 in April 1981.

On repaint, the Leyland Nationals received white bands as illustrated by No. 360 seen right in Vulcans Lane, Workington on 15th April 1981. This brought about a great improvement in appearance but it was to be short lived as we shall see later.

Displaying the NATIONAL white coach livery as it leaves Workington bus station for Whitehaven, operating service 34 from Keswick on 15th April 1980, is Duple-bodied Leyland Leopard No. 615.

The first rear-engined double-deck vehicles to enter the fleet were six Bristol VRT models with Gardner engines which arrived in1975 and were numbered 400-5. Number 401 was photographed in Main Street, St. Bees in July 1983. Despite the destination display, it was actually returning to Whitehaven.

Leaving Workington bus station for one of the many Cliftons which there are in the country, is early Bristol RE No. 253 on 23rd May 1981. It is in NBC livery with white band and is being followed by a Bristol VR double-decker heading for Seaton.

An edict was received from National Bus Company that on repaint, the white bands were to be omitted from single-deck vehicles in order to save a few pounds. This had the effect of making an already drab livery look even more drab as illustrated by Bristol RE No. 277 as it turns from Scotch Street, into Lowther Street Whitehaven, also on 23rd May 1981.

The dual-purpose vehicles were allowed to continue in the half-and-half livery as illustrated by Bristol RE No. 298 as it travels along Flatt Walks, Whitehaven on 12th August 1981. In the background is Whitehaven Castle which for many years served as the town's hospital. It then lay derelict before being renovated as residential accommodation.

The Leyland National B-type was introduced as an alternative and less sophisticated version of the original vehicle, lacking the air conditioning, for example, and Cumberland purchased 15 numbered 201-5 in 1978/9. They became known locally as the 'Country Cousins'. Photographed in Cockermouth Main Street on 1st June 1981 is No 215.

Close examination will show that these two Bristol REs, although they look different, carry the same registration number. The left hand photograph shows No. 271 turning from Whitehaven Scotch Street into Lowther Street on 25th May 1981 in its original condition. The right hand photograph shows the same bus entering George Street, Whitehaven, in July 1983, after rebuilding the front to incorporate the later double curvature windscreen. It was an expensive exercise which was not repeated.

Looking as though it is on the top of the world, Bristol VRT No. 435 passes the steep hill sign as it climbs out of Whitehaven towards Scilly Banks *en route* to Moresby Parks. The Gardner engine would no doubt cope very well with the climb.

The Leyland National 2 was a much better vehicle than the National 1 and the first examples entered the Cumberland fleet in 1980 as Nos. 370-8. A fundamental difference was the abandonment of the 500 series engine and the substitution of the Leyland O.680 engine. Photographed at Keswick during layover on the Whitehaven service, on 15th April 1981, is No. 378 with two of the withdrawn Bristol FLF double-deckers. At the right hand side is withdrawn Bristol LH No. 106 which was the first ECW body to be fitted with the double curvature windscreen and which was exhibited at the 1970 Commercial Motor Show. Number 378 is now preserved.

Bristol VRTs numbered 407-416 received between 1976 and 1978 had the Leyland 500 series engines rather than the more popular Gardner. Number 411 from this batch was photographed in Egremont Main Street in July 1983, heading for Sellafield on a Works Service. It was being followed by Willowbrook-bodied Leyland Leopard No. 628 which, by this time, had received the red and white local coach livery. In the background is Bristol RE No. 298.

Leaving a deserted Keswick bus station departing for Whitehaven and Frizington on a glorious morning in June 1981 is VRT No. 416. In the distance is the high ground of Cat Bells, over which there is an excellent walk, affording from the summit, astounding views of Borrowdale, Derwentwater, Skiddaw, Bassenthwaite Lake and the Newlands Valley.

A number of operators had asked Leyland to offer the Gardner engine as an alternative for the Leyland National 2 but had been told that 'it would not fit'. Two operators took Gardner engines which had been removed from withdrawn vehicles and fitted them to Leyland Nationals. Following this, Leyland offered the Gardner as an alternative and the first Leyland National 2 to be supplied new with a Gardner engine was Cumberland No. 395. It is shown here approaching Wath Brow on the return journey from Arlecdon to Whitehaven in July 1983. The Ennerdale Valley is in the background of the photograph below.

The Bristol VRTs were used on town and local services as well as on the longer distance routes. The photograph above shows No. 420 at George Street, Whitehaven on 29th May 1980. All later VRTs from 417 to 437 inclusive were supplied with Gardner engines. The shop on the corner at the left hand side of the photograph was for many years owned by Mr TS Bell, an electrical retailer and contractor. Mr Bell was one of the original directors of the Whitehaven Motor Service Co.

A peep behind the scenes. This photograph taken in the body shop at Whitehaven in June 1984 shows the extensive rebuilding required on the Duple Dominant body of Leyland Leopard No. 615 when it was only seven years old. It was typical of the problems encountered with these bodies. When an attempt was made to undertake similar work on No 618, it was abandoned, the body was scrapped and the chassis sold. Duple were not alone in their problems at this time; the ECW dual-purpose Leopards were fitted with what became known as a detachable boot due to its propensity to fall out of the bodywork completely. Windscreens failed similarly and these were not the coachbuilders's finest hours.

As vehicles became longer, the restrictive Seascale railway arch became a problem. A number of short Leyland Leopards were purchased from Midland Red to deal with this and they were followed by a number of similar coaches from Trent Motor Traction Company. The photographs show ex-Trent No. 606 passing through the arch in May 1984. At the other side of the arch is a sharp left hand bend.

With its involvement in National Express workings, the company had built up quite a large fleet of coaches and these were used on occasions on local services. Eastern Coach Works-bodied Leyland Leopard No. 636 was seen below, passing through Cockermouth in August 1983 whilst operating on service 34 from Keswick to Whitehaven. These coaches were given mountain names with picture which is visible on the side of the coach above the 'Cumberland' name. Number 636 was named 'Skiddaw'.

SEASCALE
MILLOM
NETHERWASDALE

Another low bridge problem. It is said that 'a little knowledge is dangerous'. The driver who collected No. 436 from the body shop in Whitehaven had a little knowledge – he thought he knew of a short cut and this was the result. Due to the gradient of the road the headroom on the town centre side of the bridge is greater than the 11ft 0in indicated on the other side. The advert on the side of the bus seems appropriate in the circumstances. (BKP)

Leyland National No. 356 travels out of Cleator Moor towards Whitehaven on the road which would have been used by the first bus service operated by Whitehaven Motor Service Company in 1914. In the background is the hill Dent, a well known landmark in the area.

The attractive West Cumbrian village of Beckermet forms the background to this view in July 1983 of Bristol VRT No. 432 as it makes its way from Seascale to Whitehaven.

The successor to the Bristol VRT was the Leyland Olympian, and Cumberland received two examples in 1983 numbered 801/2. Both were later fitted with coach seats and repainted in 'Border Clipper' livery. This view, left, shows No. 802 in original NBC livery, leaving Whitehaven for Carlisle in July 1983.

When Mr Barry Hinkley joined the company as Chief Engineer, he instigated the reinstatement of white bands on single-deck vehicles with a consequent improvement in appearance. Leyland National B type No. 208 displays this at Ennerdale bridge on 9th July 1987.

Border Clipper

Border Clipper was launched as a limited stop service between West Cumbria and Carlisle operating either via Maryport as service 300 or via Cockermouth as service 600. The launch to the press took place on 21st August 1984 at the parking area of Whitehaven Depot using Willowbrook-bodied Leyland Leopard No. 629 looking resplendent in the new livery designed for the service. There was to be one journey per day extended to the North East, initially to Sunderland, hence the destination display. The seating in these coaches was not considered suitable for long distance National Express services but was adequate for this duty.

After rebuilding of its Duple Dominant body, No. 619 was painted in Border Clipper livery and was photographed below left in Strand Street, Whitehaven, heading for Carlisle on 30th May 1986.
So popular was the Border Clipper service that the two Leyland Olympians, Nos. 801 and 802, were fitted with coach seats, renumbered 1001 and1002 and painted in Border Clipper livery. The first of the pair is shown above, photographed at Richmond, Whitehaven heading for Egremont via Cleator Moor on 30th July 1986.
An extension of the Border Clipper operation was introduced between Keswick and Carlisle using ex -rent Leyland Leopard No. 609 which received Border Clipper livery and was photographed at Bassenthwaite, returning to Keswick on 15th July 1986, below right.

Expansion North and East

In preparation for the privatisation of the National Bus Company, the government wanted to reduce the size of the larger subsidiaries such as Ribble, in order to make them more attractive to private buyers. As part of this policy the Carlisle and Penrith area of Ribble was transferred to Cumberland with effect from 23rd February 1986. This extended the Cumberland operating area as far as Newcastle upon Tyne, as Ribble had operated the Carlisle to Newcastle service jointly with United Automobile Services. The change also brought the profitable Carlisle City Services to Cumberland.

Included in the 74 vehicles transferred from Ribble was a number of full-height Bristol VRTs with Eastern Coach Works bodies similar to No. 1453 photographed in English Street, Carlisle in September 1986. The name CARLISLEBUS was adopted for buses operating on City Services.

Former Ribble Leyland National 2 No. 895 is seen at the right in Penrith in September 1986. The vehicles transferred from Ribble retained their Ribble fleet numbers on transfer to Cumberland.

Bristol VRT No. 407, seen left, from the original Cumberland fleet, and allocated to Whitehaven, was operating from Carlisle depot when photographed in the North Cumbrian town of Brampton in September 1987. Prior to the takeover of the Carlisle area from Ribble, Cumberland vehicles had not served the town of Brampton. (RD)

Ribble had operated a number of ECW-bodied Leyland Atlanteans from Carlisle and these were included in the takeover, thus bringing Leyland Atlanteans into the Cumberland fleet for the first time. Shown heading south from the city centre in September 1986 is No. 1471, displaying the CARLISLEBUS fleet name.

A New Livery

≡ cms Cumberland ≡

With the impending privatisation of the National Bus Company, subsidiary companies were released from the requirement to rigidly utilise the NBC livery and were free to develop their own distinctive colour schemes. Cumberland developed a livery of Ayres Red and Sandstone with a brown skirt and applied this in conjunction with a new fleet name which incorporated the long used local identity of CMS. The fleetname became CMS Cumberland with CMS Carlislebus being used for Carlisle City Services.

The first vehicle to receive the new livery was ECW-bodied Leyland Leopard coach No. 635, above, which received the dual-purpose version in July 1986. It is shown here at Middle Walk, Blackpool in September 1987 when it was used to transport participants and guests for the 'Driver of the Year' competition. In 1983 Roger Burge of Workington Depot won this competition and in 1984 the winner was Roy Blaikie, also from Workington Depot.

The first double-deck to receive the new livery, also in July 1986, was Bristol VRT No. 435 seen left, which, despite having been fitted with coach seating, received the standard bus version of the livery. It looked very smart in this livery as it left Carlisle for Whitehaven on 29th April 1987. (RD)

The new livery soon began to emerge in its various forms. Leyland National 2 No. 373 shows the single-deck service bus style as it leaves Workington bus station in April 1987 making for Seaton. (BKP)

The dual-purpose version of the livery, as applied to coach-seated Leyland Nationals, is displayed by No. 382, as it crosses from Strand Street into Tangier Street, Whitehaven on 9th July 1987. Although fitted with coach seats, the vehicle was operating on a Town Service when photographed. In the background is another Whitehaven landmark which no longer exists. This was the conveyor system which was used to convey phosphate rock from ships to the storage silos on the dock side.

The Minibus Arrives

Minibus operation commenced in Whitehaven and Workington on Monday 27th October 1986, the first operational day after deregulation.

On the first day of operation the weather was dark, damp and dismal when the first minibuses commenced operation on Town Services 01 and 02 in Whitehaven and on Town Services 50 and 51 in Workington. The photographs left and above show numbers 25 and 26 in Whitehaven on that first day. The vehicles were Dodge 56 with Reeve Burgess coachbuilt (as distinct from van conversion) bodies. The destination blinds were of yellow background with small black lettering displaying the route and not just the final destination.

On a much brighter day, 23rd September 1988, No. 22 leaves Workington bus station for Seaton. By this time minibus operation had been extended and, in Workington, included service 47.

Minibus operation commenced in Carlisle on 9th February 1987 with two services, M3 and M4. The vehicles were Mercedes-Benz L608D models with van conversion bodies by Reeve Burgess. Photographed in English Street, Carlisle on 28th August 1987 is No. 42.

22nd July 1987 – The Last Day of National Bus Company Ownership

At 8.45am with mist hanging over Skiddaw, No. 204 enters Keswick on service 35 from Brathay Hill with service number indicator already set for the 9.15am departure on service 79 to Seatoller.

With its white livery contrasting against the overcast sky, Duple Laser-bodied Leyland Tiger No. 107 leaves Keswick bus station on the Whitehaven to London service of National Express.

Later in the same day, passing through Howgate is coach-seated Bristol VRT No. 436 displaying a dual-purpose version of the new livery. It was *en route* from Broughton Moor to Whitehaven on service 31.

In an attempt to counter competition from Brownriggs, a number of coaches were painted in all-white livery and operated with 'Bargain Bus' cards in the windscreen together with another card declaring the destination. One such coach was Duple-bodied Leyland Leopard No. 1119 shown here in Duke Street, Whitehaven, heading for 'Thornhill via Bigrigg'.

Cumberland

PART OF THE STAGECOACH GROUP

As part of the privatisation policy, Cumberland was sold to Stagecoach Holdings and the first day of operation under the new owners was 23rd July 1987. Initially there were early changes to the management structure but no outward signs of change visible to passengers. Vehicles continued to be painted in the new livery.

In August 1987 Leyland National 2 No. 377 was photographed turning from Duke Street into Scotch Street, Whitehaven *en route* to Egremont.

Border Clipper services continued as evidenced by Willowbrook-bodied Leyland Leopard No. 628 seen below displaying the later 'Border Clipper' style brand name as it travels along Duke Street, Whitehaven in August 1987.

Crossing Citadel Square, Carlisle on 28th August 1987 is full-height Bristol VRT No. 1450. This was a scene which was soon to change as all 17 Bristol VRTs inherited from Ribble with the Carlisle operation were transferred by Stagecoach to another of its subsidiaries, Hampshire Bus. In exchange Cumberland received a variety of vehicles, mainly Leyland Fleetline DMS models. Four Ailsa B55-10 double-deckers involved in the deal had very short lives with Cumberland. At the end of September, the 17 Bristol VRTs were driven by Carlisle drivers to Knutsford Services on the M6 motorway and exchanged,with the vehicles brought north driven by Hampshire Bus drivers.

Competition in Whitehaven continued as illustrated by this view in George Street in August 1987. Yeowarts Optare-bodied Leyland Cub operating on Town Service Y2 is followed by a Brownrigg's Leyland Leopard operating to Frizington.

Arriving from Whitehaven on 5th November 1987, Leyland National 2 No. 384 passes along English street displaying the new livery.

One of the ex-Hampshire Bus Leyland Fleetlines received in exchange for the Bristol VRTs was No. 1918 shown below in Lowther Street, Carlisle on 5th November 1987.

Cumberland took over the Yeowart operation with effect from 12th May 1988 and in July 1988 a Leyland National 1, No. 358 and two Leyland National B types Nos. 216 and 218 were painted in the Yeowart livery for operation on former Yeowart services. Pictured in Duke Street Whitehaven on 5th August 1988 is No. 216 operating on Town Service Y2.

At 8am on 9th May 1990, Leyland National B type No. 210 was photographed at Ravenglass, passing under the railway bridge which carries the Ravenglass and Eskdale Railway. Behind is another bridge carrying the Cumbrian Coast main railway line. This bus is now preserved.

Urban and Rural Scenes in 1988 and 1989

A scene in Lowther Street, Whitehaven in August 1988 shows Leyland National 2 No. 387 overtaking minibus No. 26 as it loads for Town Service 08. Behind is another Leyland National 2. Number 387 was operating on Haven Link service 9-7. The Haven Link services had been introduced following competition from Yeowarts and linked together various Town Services. Another view of No. 387 is shown at the page foot in an entirely different setting.

Gardner-engined Bristol VRT No. 418 leaves Workington bus station for Whitehaven operating service 30 from Carlisle on 23rd September 1988.

Operating service 35 from Keswick to Whitehaven and Frizington on 19th May 1989, Bristol VRT No. 435 crosses Ouse Bridge, Bassenthwaite.

Another bridge scene, this time in rural West Cumbria. Leyland National 2 No. 387 approaches the bridge at Wath Brow over the river Ehen, *en route* from Whitehaven to Ennerdale on 5th August 1988.

Arrival of the Routemasters

An early event following the takeover by Stagecoach was the purchase of eight ex-London Transport Routemasters for service in Carlisle on City Service 61. The vehicles were numbered 900-907 and were prepared for service at Whitehaven as shown here with two of them, Nos. 900 and 902, in Central Works on 25th September 1987. They were painted in their own version of the CMS Cumberland livery.

Photographed in the City Centre on 9th September 1988 is No. 906 awaiting departure to Harraby East.

Crossing Citadel Square, having emerged from Botchergate and heading for Morton Park on 21st April 1989, is No. 902.

Expansion to the South

Stagecoach, having taken over Ribble Motor Services as from 21st April 1989, announced that with effect from 18th June 1989 the South Lakes and Furness areas of Ribble would be transferred to Cumberland. This meant that the company now covered the whole of the County of Cumbria.

This expansion brought to Cumberland operation of the 555 trunk service from Keswick to Lancaster which had been operated from Kendal Depot. The photograph shows Bristol VRT No. 423 which, along with sister vehicle No. 422, had been transferred from Whitehaven for operation under the Arnside railway bridge. Entering Ambleside in November 1990 it is seen on the 555 service from Lancaster to Keswick.

Another area of operation was the Langdale Valley and services to Coniston. On a glorious autumn morning of 10th November 1999, Plaxton-bodied Leyland Leopard No. 1199 had just left Elterwater for the return journey to Ambleside.

Town services in Kendal were a significant part of the operation and Mercedes 608 minibus No. 5041 is shown opposite the bus station operating on a Town Service. It had been numbered 504 in the Ribble fleet but there was already a vehicle numbered 504 in the Cumberland fleet so a '1' was added making it 5041 – the highest number ever applied to a Cumberland vehicle prior to the introduction of the comprehensive Stagecoach numbering system.

Ribble had taken over the operation of Barrow Borough Transport including a number of vehicles. Former Barrow Transport Leyland National 1 NEO 830R had received 'Cumberland' fleetnames when photographed at Ramsden Square, Barrow in July 1989 carrying fleet number 757.

The Stagecoach Standard Leyland Olympian

The Alexander-bodied Leyland Olympian became the standard Stagecoach double-deck vehicle for a number of years. The first examples for Cumberland arrived in September 1988 and comprised a batch of nine, numbered 1003-11. They were allocated to Carlisle where they were used mainly on City Services. This photograph taken on 21st April 1989 in English Street, shows No. 1105 with back to the camera and No. 1106 facing the camera. In the background is a Routemaster.

A change in body specification was made for the next batch in that twin destination blinds were fitted, allowing display of intermediate points. These were short lived, however, and were replaced by Hanover electronically operated displays which were also retrofitted to earlier Olympians. The entire batch numbered 1020-7 was allocated to Kendal for the 555 service. Shown arriving at Windermere, below, with its original destination display on 29th July 1992 is No. 1021, operating the 09.15hrs service from Ambleside to Lancaster. Coming through on the nearside is Plaxton-bodied Bedford C321 PRM from the immaculate fleet of Syd Rae of Whitehaven.

The second batch of Olympians were numbered 1012–9, arriving in August 1990, and with the exception of No. 1019 which was allocated to Kendal, were allocated to Whitehaven and Workington. The photograph above shows No. 1012 leaving Whitehaven bus station for Thornhill on 25th October 1990.

The final batch of Olympians numbered 1028-35 arrived in October 1992 and differed from earlier examples in that they were shorter, a fact that is evident from the lack of a short bay in the centre of the body. Shown arriving in Carlisle bus station from Longtown on 24th May 1997 is No. 1033.

A view taken in English Street, Carlisle, shortly after that on the previous page shows a variety of vehicles and liveries. Routemaster No. 905 and Leyland National 2 No. 302 head away from the camera whilst a National 1, No. 756, still in NBC livery, faces the camera followed by a Leyland Atlantean in the CMS Cumberland livery.

Leyland National 1s were never regular performers on service 30 Whitehaven to Carlisle and it was surprising to find No. 365 leaving Carlisle for Whitehaven on 21st April 1989 when it was 14½ years old.

A view in Cockermouth Main Street on 15th May 1990 shows No. 431 leaving the town for Carlisle on Border Clipper Service 600. By this time vehicles in standard liveries were being used on Border Clipper services. This particular vehicle is now preserved.

Kendal Depot had a need for the 13ft 5ins high version of the Bristol VRT for operation under the railway bridge on the Arnside service. The two Ribble vehicles previously used for this were transferred elsewhere by Ribble on the takeover by Cumberland. Arising from this, VRTs Nos. 422 and 423 were transferred to Kendal, the former being in CMS Cumberland livery as displayed here in Milnthorpe on 24th April 1990.

A 1991 Tour

At the request of Stagecoach, the author undertook a tour of the depots and operating area in August 1991 to produce a series of photographs. A selection of these is included in the next five pages and these indicate the variety of vehicle and liveries in use at that time.

WHITEHAVEN

A good starting point was Head Office, next to the bus station in Whitehaven, which had been built in 1931. It remained as Head Office until 24th May 1999 when it became Stagecoach Holdings Divisional Office. As a result of this and the inability to find alternative accommodation in West Cumbria, the Head Office for Cumberland Motor Services was moved to rented accommodation in Broadacre House, Lowther Street, Carlisle. Following further reorganisation in the Group, all administration was centred on Perth and the Whitehaven Office closed at the end of August 2000.

An internal view of Whitehaven's refurbished bus station which had recently been completed. Awaiting departure to Carlisle on Border Clipper Service 600 below is No. 1201, one of two 6 wheel 'Megadekkas' in the fleet. Each was provided with 96 coach seats in the Alexander-built body, with the chassis being a lengthened version of the popular Leyland Olympian.

A view of the body shop on Wellington Row, Whitehaven, above, with a Plaxton-bodied Leyland Leopard and a Bristol VRT receiving attention. The paint shop was through the body shop to the right. As vehicles became longer, access to these premises became increasingly difficult.

Travelling along Scotch Street, Whitehaven is minibus No. 28 which, by this time, had received Stagecoach livery.

WORKINGTON

Workington's historic bus station was, by this time, looking somewhat shabby – so much so that it was awarded the 'Broken Gnome Award' for the most dilapidated building in town by the local council. Stagecoach responded to this and carried out a major refurbishment programme similar to that carried out at Whitehaven and which was completed for reopening on 22nd June 1993. Loading for Town Service 46 is National 2 No. 384 in dual-purpose livery.

Metrorider No. 91 was one of two taken over from Brownriggs and it is shown in Vulcans Lane outside the Workington Depot building.

Leyland Olympian No. 1015 had just emerged from the rear of the bus station into Vulcans Lane *en route* from Whitehaven to Carlisle.

WIGTON

Wigton bus station was still in use at this time and Willowbrook-bodied Leyland Leopard No. 630, which had previously carried Border Clipper livery, was operating on Border Clipper service 300 to Carlisle having been repainted into standard Stagecoach livery.

Travelling through Main Street, Wigton on service 30 from Carlisle to Whitehaven is Leyland National 2 number 379.

1991 Tour – 3

CARLISLE

Varied vehicles and liveries in Carlisle bus station. Duple-bodied Leyland Tiger No. 156 awaits departure to Newcastle upon Tyne in the current version of 'Coachline' livery which was based on the livery of Yeowarts Coaches, Whitehaven which had been taken over. Alongside, a Bristol VRT awaits departure to Silloth.

Little and large in Citadel Square, below. Minibus No. 63 in Citadel Square with a Leyland Olympian proceeding up Botchergate.

Routemasters were still in evidence with No. 903 proceeding along The Crescent. In the background a Leyland National 2 follows with an Olympian behind it.

MILLOM

At the other end of the county, in Millom Square, minibus No. 70 awaits departure on the local service to Haverigg.

1991 Tour – 4

KENDAL

Eastern Coach Works-bodied Leyland Atlantean No. 1471 which had previously operated in Carlisle had now received Stagecoach livery and was photographed leaving Kendal bus station for Keswick, a service normally operated by coach-seated Olympians.

National Express operations continued and at this time there was a daily service from Whitehaven to Leeds which, on this occasion, was being operated by ex-Hampshire Bus Plaxton-bodied Leyland Tiger No. 111. A Kendal driver joined the coach at this point to drive from Forton Services to Leeds and return, the Whitehaven driver leaving at that point to take up other duties. The author recalls a conversation with the Kendal driver who stated that, on the previous day he had arrived at Chorlton Street, Manchester where 'as usual there was chaos', so much so that he said to the inspector 'It's time someone put a bomb under this place'. On return from Leeds later in the day, the station was closed because of a bomb scare!

Tourist services in the central area of the Lake District formed, and still form, an important part of operations from Kendal Depot. This photograph at Bowness on Windermere shows minibus No. 558 and ex-Portsmouth City Transport open-top Atlantean No. 1928 awaiting departure to Coniston and Ambleside.

KESWICK

A mixed scene at Keswick bus station shows Leyland National 2 No. 375 still in NBC livery on Service 35 to Whitehaven and Frizington. To the left of the photograph is Olympian 1001 awaiting departure on Service 555 to Lancaster. The coach in the middle was from another operator, being used to duplicate Cumberland No. 108, at this point hidden from view behind No. 1001, on the Whitehaven to London service.

1991 Tour – 5

KESWICK

Having left Keswick bus station Bristol VRT No. 417 makes its way alongside Bassenthwaite Lake (the only lake in the Lake District which is officially called a lake, the others being . . . water or . . . mere.)

BARROW IN FURNESS

At this time Barrow Depot still occupied the premises formerly owned by Barrow Borough Transport which were somewhat dilapidated and were soon to be replaced by new premises where conditions would be a considerable improvement on those seen here. The photograph shows a Leyland National 2, still in the Ribble post privatisation livery but with Cumberland fleetname, together with a National 2 and a Mercedes minibus, both in Stagecoach livery.

Abbey Road provides an attractive entrance into the town of Barrow in Furness and the photograph shows ex-Ribble Leyland National 2 No. 857 on this road, passing the town's Railway Station.

At this time the Leyland Lynx vehicles were allocated to Barrow, and No. 251 is shown far from home, emerging from Grasmere village on to the main road whilst operating the Ulverston to Grasmere service. This vehicle is now preserved.

Contrasting Scenes and Liveries – August 1991

As previously mentioned, there were three main liveries in use at this time, apart from those on coaches and National Express vehicles. Readers will no doubt have their own opinion on these liveries.

Seen at Bassenthwaite, with the Skiddaw range in the background, is No. 2032, one of the Bristol VRTs taken over with the Carlisle and Penrith operations of Ribble. The fact that this vehicle was 13ft 8in mid-height, as distinct from those new to Cumberland which were all the low 13ft 5in high versions, is evident from the narrow white band above the windscreen.

On the last stage of its journey from Keswick to the village of Frizington, No. 421 turns from Scotch Street into Lowther Street, Whitehaven with the Union Hall in the background. It is in the CMS Cumberland livery introduced in 1986 in preparation for privatisation.

Leaving Workington's historic bus station, also *en route* to Frizington, and carrying Stagecoach livery, is No. 425. It will be noted from this and other photographs, that when Stagecoach livery was first applied the Cumberland fleetname was retained.

The Arrival of the Midibus

Following extensive use of minibuses in recent years, it became clear that many operators would welcome something in between the size of the minibus and full size single-deck vehicles. Dennis responded to this by introducing their 'Dart' rear engine model and it became very popular with all sizes of operator. Cumberland received three numbered 701-3 and No. 702 is shown at George Street, Whitehaven operating on Town Service 07 to Mirehouse Estate in May 1992. All three Darts were later transferred to another Stagecoach company.

Volvo then decided to do something about this and introduced their B6 model to compete with the Dennis Dart. Cumberland ordered 100 of these and the first one, No. 704, was delivered in time to convey guests on the occasion of the official opening of Lillyhall Depot on 26th June 1992. It is shown, right, on the dockside at Whitehaven earlier in the day. The publicity material for the opening contained reference to the merits of these vehicles. Unfortunately, they did not live up to expectations, this one failed *en route* from the body builders to Whitehaven and this unreliability was repeated in all five initial vehicles. Arising from this, Cumberland returned all five to Volvo, who subsequently replaced them. In the meantime Volvo temporarily withdrew the model and Cumberland cancelled their order, replacing it with an order for the tried and tested Volvo B10M.

Among the replacement Volvo B6 models were No. 279 shown here leaving Workington bus station in September 1993 and No. 274 shown entering Duke Street, Whitehaven also in September 1993.

The Volvo B10M

The first examples of the B10M arrived in December 1992 and were allocated to Carlisle. They became versatile vehicles, used on a variety of services and No. 734 is shown above on 26th July 1995 in Lowther Street, Carlisle operating on City Service 68 as Alexander-bodied Mercedes minibus 85 travels in the opposite direction.

The next B10Ms were allocated to Barrow and No. 755 was photographed at Rampside on 10th July 1995 returning from Ulverston to Barrow via the Coast Road. As mentioned earlier, the Volvo B10M with Alexander body arrived in the fleet by default following dissatisfaction with the Volvo B6. Some sharp-eyed readers may recognise the parked car, registered K2 POS.

After Carlisle and Barrow, West Cumbria received an allocation of B10M models and again they were used on a variety of services. Shown in Strand Street, Whitehaven on 31st August 1994 is No. 770 operating on Haven Link Service 7-9. In the background a Mercedes 608 minibus descends Rosemary Lane on Town Service 01.

On a glorious Spring day, 25th May 1999, No. 751 returns from Carlisle to Whitehaven on service 300 and was photographed at Lillyhall. The entrance to the former Leyland National factory is on the right and Lillyhall depot is on the other side of the road.

Later, B10M models were allocated to Kendal Depot and No. 774 was leaving Ambleside for Langdale and Dungeon Ghyll in June 2001.

Bristol VRT No. 437 was numerically the last VRT to be delivered new to Cumberland and was almost 14 years old when photographed in March 1994 turning from Duke Street into Scotch Street, Whitehaven. It was, as usual, well turned out.

Standing in Cleator Moor Square in September 1996, possibly in the place or near the place of the terminus of the first bus service from Whitehaven to Cleator Moor in 1914, is Mercedes minibus No. 26. It was heading for Arlecdon, having travelled via the West Cumberland Hospital in Whitehaven. The shop in the background, occupied by 'Paul's Wines', was for many years the waiting room and parcels office for Cumberland Motor Services.

Over at the other side of the county, a Plaxton-bodied Leyland Leopard approaches the top of Kirkstone Pass in this early morning view on 18th August 1997. The sun catches Lake Windermere in the valley below.

Contrasting Scenes in 1999

Despite being 19 years old, Bristol VRT looked immaculate when photographed at Glenridding on 20th July 1999 whilst operating the Penrith to Patterdale service. Brilliant white vehicles in intensely strong sunshine against vivid blue sky and misty mountain backscenes can make for challenging pictures but once again the beauty of the lakes is clear for all to see.

In 1999 Carlisle received ten MAN 18.220 low-floor single-deckers with Alexander bodies, becoming numbers 801-4/6-9/11-12. Pictured in the city on 2nd October 1999 is No. 804 operating on a city service to Morton Park. In early January 2005 Carlisle suffered extensive flooding which embraced the depot at Willowholme. The result of this was that the entire Carlisle fleet, with the exception of vehicles outstationed at Penrith, suffered extensive damage. Vehicles were brought in from other Stagecoach operators to maintain the service and 39 new Dennis Darts were purchased as replacements, two of which can be seen on page 66.

Leaving Carlisle bus station for Newcastle upon Tyne on 2nd August 1999 is Plaxton-bodied Volvo B10M coach No. 792 carrying the special livery for this service which was also carried by Arriva vehicles, with whom the service was jointly operated. The double-decker behind very clearly demonstrates the method by which Alexander lengthened the body, with the addition of a spliced-in extra bay.

At the other end of the county in Barrow in Furness a number of Mercedes Vario 0814 larger minibuses, seating 29 passengers in their Alexander bodies, had arrived the previous year. One of these, No. 92, was photographed in Abbey Road, Barrow on 23rd August 1999.

Some Rural Scenes in West Cumbria in July 1999

Mercedes minibus No. 33 passes through Ennerdale Bridge whilst operating service 219 from Cockermouth to Cleator Moor.

A little later on the same day similar minibus No. 27 was photographed passing through Sandwith *en route* from Whitehaven to St Bees on service 20. Sandwith, although rural in character was, until local government reorganisation in 1974, part of the Borough of Whitehaven.

Further south, Volvo B10M No. 748 is shown having just left the village of Holmrook heading for Ravenglass on service 6 from Whitehaven.

With Lakeland Hills in the background, minibus No. 57 arrives in the village of Haverigg on the local service from Millom.

A New Millennium – A New Livery

Stagecoach introduced a new livery still incorporating, white, blue, orange and red but applied in a completely different way to the previous livery. Vehicles of all types began appearing in this livery in 2001.

Minibus No. 61 had received the new livery when photographed entering George Street, Whitehaven on 22nd June 2001. Facing the camera is the boarded up Central Works which has since become a Wetherspoons establishment. On the other side of Tangier Street is the former Whitehaven Depot building, often referred to as the '1932 Workshops'. It closed with the opening of Lillyhall and at the time of writing remains unoccupied.

Volvo B10M No. 776 was carrying the new livery when photographed at Glenridding in August 2002. It had just turned and was heading back to Bowness on Windermere via Kirkstone Pass.

Even the Lake District open-top double-deckers received the new livery as shown by Leyland Titan No. 10281 in May 2008, as it passes Nab Cottage, Rydal with Rydal Water on the other side. The fleet number was that applied with the advent of the Stagecoach comprehensive fleet numbering system.

Two vehicles demonstrate the new livery at Keswick bus station in August 2002. Leyland Olympian No. 2281 was commencing the long journey to Lancaster on service 555 with a young man occupying a favourite but potentially dangerous position for people of his generation, standing at the front of the upper saloon. Alongside and awaiting departure to Penrith on service X50 is MAN No. 801.

The X4/X5/X50

The X4/X5 services were introduced on 16th May 1993 with the basic service operating between Whitehaven and Penrith with some extensions to and from Carlisle and also to and from Langwathby. These extensions were short-lived and not repeated the following year. Volvo B10M No. 778 was photographed in Keswick bus station in July 1997 loading for Whitehaven.

With the introduction of the Jonckheere-bodied Volvo B10M coaches in 1998, the service was curtailed to operate only between Workington and Penrith. On 30th July 2001, No. 799 was photographed at Braithwaite having had to cross to the other side of the road to avoid parked cars near the junction. It was carrying 'Cumbria Connexion' livery.

Also carrying 'Cumbria Connexion' livery when photographed in Keswick bus station in June 2001 was MAN No. 813 operating the short working X50 between Keswick and Penrith. As from 2011 all workings on the service between Keswick and Penrith are numbered X50 but no change of vehicle is required and through booking can be made to and from places west of Keswick.

Carrying 'Trans Cumbria' route branding on its Stagecoach livery, No. 53337, a Plaxton-bodied Volvo B10M, turns off the A66 to call at Threlkeld on 8th January 2010. (DMcA)

Route Branding

In 2006 Cumbria County Council purchased three Dennis Tridents bodied by East Lancashire Coachbuilders and had them finished in a special livery and route branded for the X35 service between Barrow in Furness and Kendal. Operated by Stagecoach they were launched at Haverthwaite Railway Station on 28th February 2006. They carried Cumberland Motor Services legal lettering, the first new East Lancashire bodies to do so since 1941.

One of the Dennis Tridents, No. 18278 was photographed leaving Grange over Sands for Kendal on 27th September 2010. (MB)

In 2008 a fleet of eleven MAN 18.240 models with ADL Enviro 300 bodies was purchased for the Maryport – Workington – Whitehaven – Thornhill (30) / Frizington (31) services which incorporated the 17/17A service. Workington's new temporary bridge was opened on 21st April 2010 and the following day No. 22609 operating from Maryport to Thornhill was photographed as it turned on to the replacement structure.
The remains of the destroyed Northside bridge can be seen down river. (DMcA)

Whitehaven in the 21st Century

Double-deck vehicles, which once predominated in the Cumberland fleet, are now in the minority but still to be seen. Travelling along Duke Street, Whitehaven, on a sunny day in April 2007, Leyland Olympian No. 14255 was well turned out in the latest livery as it headed towards Lowther Street to commence its journey to Moresby Parks. It was passing minibus No. 40028 which was picking up passengers on Town Service 2 to Woodhouse and Greenbank.

An Optare Versa model was purchased and route branded for Whitehaven Town Service 2. It is shown at Woodhouse Estate on 18th August 2008. However, it was not considered suitable for this particular route and it was transferred to another area of Stagecoach. (DMcA)

The Mercedes minibuses were replaced by larger Optare Solo models and No. 47617 was photographed on a wet day, 21st August 2008, in Strand Street, Whitehaven, operating on Town Service 3 – Mirehouse Circular. (DMcA)

After the departure of the Optare Versa, the operation of Town Service 2 was taken over by ADL Dennis Darts and No. 35249 is shown climbing Kells New Road, on 20th August 2008, heading for Woodhouse and Greenbank. (DMcA)

Workington in the 21st Century

Many parts of Cumbria suffered flooding in November 2009, but Workington was probably affected more than any other area. Northside Bridge was swept away with the tragic loss of PC Bill Barker who was on the bridge at the time. In addition the Calva Bridge was declared unsafe with the result that the town was divided in two, having a severe effect on North-South traffic. On the morning of the floods, two Stagecoach inspectors – Kevin Sheehan and David Hoare – performed a magnificent job, directing traffic and pedestrians away from the affected crossings. Their actions were later acknowledged with Royal Humane Society Awards and the Chief Constable's Award. The situation had a major effect on bus services with modified temporary services established in conjunction with a temporary railway station given the name Workington North.

A temporary footbridge was built and on 12th April 2010 MAN No. 22607 and Optare Solo No. 47005 stand on the south side of the bridge whilst Dennis Dart No. 35248 waits on the north side. (DMcA)

A temporary bridge for traffic was built and opened on 21st April 2010. Seconds after the bridge was declared open MAN No. 22607 crossed the bridge with its destination display declaring 'Workington Reconnected' watched by residents no doubt greatly relieved that their town had indeed been reconnected. (DMcA)

With the opening of the bridge, north-south bus services were re-established including the Whitehaven to Carlisle service 300. Volvo Olympian No. 16253 is shown crossing the bridge. (DMcA)

One of the MAN single-deckers, purchased specifically for services 30/31, No. 22595 is shown approaching the Curwen Park bus stop which served the footbridge on 12th April 2010. The Calva Bridge which had been declared unusable following flood damage can be seen in the background. (DMcA)

Carlisle in the 21st Century

Following the floods of January 2005, previously mentioned, Carlisle depot received 39 Dennis Darts with Alexander bodies as replacements for vehicles damaged in the floods. On a sunny day in March 2006, No. 34700 was photographed leaving the bus station for Morton Park with a Volvo B10M in the background. These vehicles now dominate the bus scene as far as city services are concerned.

On the same day, No. 34689 overtakes Volvo B10M No. 20727 as it approaches the city centre *en route* to Harraby East. Note the 'Carlisle Citi' fleet name.

Dennis Dart No. 34719 picks up passengers opposite the Market Hall in Carlisle as Volvo Olympian No. 16653 passes on service 300 from Whitehaven on 19th July 2008. Note the display of information regarding time and next departures. (DMcA)

As night falls on 15th December 2007, Dennis Dart No. 34715 approaches the city centre *en route* to Harraby East. In the background heading out of the city is an Olympian double-decker, possibly on service 300 to Whitehaven. (DMcA)

Kendal in the 21st Century

Optare Solo No. 47009 was photographed in Kendal on 26th August 2010 operating Town Service 42A to Larch Grove. (RD)

An early morning view of Northern Counties-bodied Volvo Olympian No. 16184 shows it leaving Kendal on 24th June 2010 operating the 07.55hrs departure for Kirkby Lonsdale (RD)

Marshall-bodied Dennis Dart No. 33170 is shown leaving Kendal for Arnside at 09.15hrs on 25th August 2011. (RD)

Returning to Kendal Depot at 08.59hrs on 24th June 2010 and displaying its CMS Cumberland livery is Leyland Olympian No. 14245, which had operated the Dallam School Contract D6. (RD)

Barrow in Furness in the 21st Century

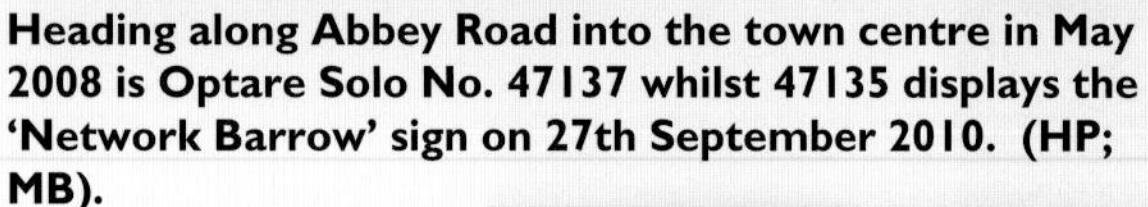

Heading along Abbey Road into the town centre in May 2008 is Optare Solo No. 47137 whilst 47135 displays the 'Network Barrow' sign on 27th September 2010. (HP; MB).

Barrow-based Alexander-bodied Leyland Olympian No. 14267 was painted in the Barrow Corporation colours of cream and dark blue. It was so attired when heading into Grange over Sands in May 2008 deputising for one of the regular vehicles on the X35 service from Barrow to Kendal.

The Arrival of the Scanias

On a damp and miserable 'summer' day 2nd August 2011 Scania No. 15683 displays its route details and brand name 'West Coast Connect' for the Whitehaven to Carlisle service as it stands below left in Carlisle bus station ready for the return journey. In the right hand view it is shown entering Lowther Street from Lonsdale Street showing the revised destination display of '300 Maryport for 302 Whitehaven'. This followed the splitting of the 300 service into two sections earlier in 2011. The same vehicle works through from Carlisle to Whitehaven, and through fares are available.

The Scanias again

Photographed leaving Maryport on 1st September 2010, when brand new, is Alexander-bodied Scania N230UD No. 15685 operating on service 300 from Whitehaven to Carlisle. (DMcA)

In September 2011 nine new Scanias entered service on the 555 route from Keswick to Lancaster, and were painted in the green version of the standard Stagecoach livery. Number 15726 was photographed on a wet Sunday 27th November 2011 at Dale Bottom heading for Keswick. (DMcA)

Cumberland in Lakeland

In addition to services to Keswick, Cumberland's operation in Lakeland prior to 1989 comprised services to Wasdale, Ennerdale, Buttermere, Ullswater and Borrowdale. Some of these were market day rather than tourist orientated.

Photographed at Buttermere in pre-war days is this 1929 Leyland TS2 No. 111 which, along with Nos. 112-4 had been rebodied by Myers and Bowman of Distington in 1938. Cov Rad radiators were fitted at the same time. It had probably operated on the service from Keswick via Whinlatter Pass. Standing behind is Leyland TS7 No. 50 with a Burlingham coach body, dating from 1936. (OS)

Leyland TS2 No. 30 dating from 1929 was rebodied by Massey Bros. with this body to coach outline but with bus seats in 1939. A Cov Rad radiator was fitted at the same time and it is shown in Keswick bus station awaiting departure to Seatoller in Borrowdale. Behind is 1936 Massey-bodied Leyland TD4 No. 118 on the service to Whitehaven. The service to Borrowdale was a complex joint operation with local operators as shown by the 1954 table seen below.

Key to Operators in Table :-
AA – Askew SS – Simpson WW – Weightman YY – Youngs CC – Cumberland

WEEKDAYS SUMMER 1954

Wk																								
1M	CC	CC	YY	WW	SS	CC	YY	WW	SS	CC	YY	WW	SS	CC	YY	WW	SS	CC	YY	WW	SS	YY	SS	
1T	AA	AA	CC	YY	WW	AA	CC	YY	WW	AA	CC	YY	WW	AA	CC	YY	WW	AA	CC	YY	WW	CC	WW	
1W	SS	SS	AA	CC	YY	SS	AA	CC	YY	SS	AA	CC	YY	SS	AA	CC	YY	SS	AA	CC	YY	AA	YY	YY
1Th	WW	WW	SS	AA	CC	WW	SS	AA	CC	WW	SS	AA	CC	WW	SS	AA	CC	WW	SS	AA	CC	SS	CC	
1F	YY	YY	WW	SS	AA	YY	WW	SS	AA	YY	WW	SS	AA	YY	WW	SS	AA	YY	WW	SS	AA	WW	AA	
1S	CC	CC	YY	WW	SS	CC	YY	WW	SS	CC	YY	WW	SS	CC	YY	WW	SS	CC	YY	WW	SS	YY	SS	SS
2M	SS	SS	AA	YY	WW	SS	AA	YY	WW	SS	AA	YY	WW	SS	AA	YY	WW	SS	AA	YY	WW	AA	WW	
2T	CC	CC	SS	AA	YY	CC	SS	AA	YY	CC	SS	AA	YY	CC	SS	AA	YY	CC	SS	AA	YY	SS	YY	
2W	WW	WW	CC	SS	AA	WW	CC	SS	AA	WW	CC	SS	AA	WW	CC	SS	AA	WW	CC	SS	AA	CC	AA	AA
2Th	YY	YY	WW	CC	SS	YY	WW	CC	SS	YY	WW	CC	SS	YY	WW	CC	SS	YY	WW	CC	SS	WW	SS	
2F	AA	AA	YY	WW	CC	AA	YY	WW	CC	AA	YY	WW	CC	AA	YY	WW	CC	AA	YY	WW	CC	YY	CC	
2S	SS	SS	AA	YY	WW	SS	AA	YY	WW	SS	AA	YY	WW	SS	AA	YY	WW	SS	AA	YY	WW	AA	WW	WW
3M	WW	WW	CC	AA	YY	WW	CC	AA	YY	WW	CC	AA	YY	WW	CC	AA	YY	WW	CC	AA	YY	CC	YY	
3T	SS	SS	WW	CC	AA	SS	WW	CC	AA	SS	WW	CC	AA	SS	WW	CC	AA	SS	WW	CC	AA	WW	AA	
3W	YY	YY	SS	WW	CC	YY	SS	WW	CC	YY	SS	WW	CC	YY	SS	WW	CC	YY	SS	WW	CC	SS	CC	CC
3Th	AA	AA	YY	SS	WW	AA	YY	SS	WW	AA	YY	SS	WW	AA	YY	SS	WW	AA	YY	SS	WW	YY	WW	
3F	CC	CC	AA	YY	SS	CC	AA	YY	SS	CC	AA	YY	SS	CC	AA	YY	SS	CC	AA	YY	SS	AA	SS	
3S	WW	WW	CC	AA	YY	WW	CC	AA	YY	WW	CC	AA	YY	WW	CC	AA	YY	WW	CC	AA	YY	CC	YY	YY
4M	YY	YY	SS	CC	AA	YY	SS	CC	AA	YY	SS	CC	AA	YY	SS	CC	AA	YY	SS	CC	AA	SS	AA	
4T	WW	WW	YY	SS	CC	WW	YY	SS	CC	WW	YY	SS	CC	WW	YY	SS	CC	WW	YY	SS	CC	YY	CC	
4W	AA	AA	WW	YY	SS	AA	WW	YY	SS	AA	WW	YY	SS	AA	WW	YY	SS	AA	WW	YY	SS	WW	SS	SS
4Th	CC	CC	AA	WW	YY	CC	AA	WW	YY	CC	AA	WW	YY	CC	AA	WW	YY	CC	AA	WW	YY	AA	YY	
4F	SS	SS	CC	AA	WW	SS	CC	AA	WW	SS	CC	AA	WW	SS	CC	AA	WW	SS	CC	AA	WW	CC	WW	
4S	YY	YY	SS	CC	AA	YY	SS	CC	AA	YY	SS	CC	AA	YY	SS	CC	AA	YY	SS	CC	AA	SS	AA	AA
5M	AA	AA	WW	SS	CC	AA	WW	SS	CC	AA	WW	SS	CC	AA	WW	SS	CC	AA	WW	SS	CC	WW	CC	
5T	YY	YY	AA	WW	SS	YY	AA	WW	SS	YY	AA	WW	SS	YY	AA	WW	SS	YY	AA	WW	SS	AA	SS	
5W	CC	CC	YY	AA	WW	CC	YY	AA	WW	CC	YY	AA	WW	CC	YY	AA	WW	CC	YY	AA	WW	YY	WW	WW
5Th	SS	SS	CC	YY	AA	SS	CC	YY	AA	SS	CC	YY	AA	SS	CC	YY	AA	SS	CC	YY	AA	CC	AA	
5F	WW	WW	SS	CC	YY	WW	SS	CC	YY	WW	SS	CC	YY	WW	SS	CC	YY	WW	SS	CC	YY	SS	YY	
5S	AA	AA	WW	SS	CC	AA	WW	SS	CC	AA	WW	SS	CC	AA	WW	SS	CC	AA	WW	SS	CC	WW	CC	CC
Keswick	0700	0815	0915	0945	1000	1020	1045	1115	1145	1230	1315	1400	1420	1440	1500	1530	1600	1620	1640	1700	1730	1800	1845	2050
Lodore Hotel		0825	0925	0950	1010	1030	1055	1125	1155	1240	1325	1410	1430	1450	1510	1540	1610	1630	1650	1710	1740	1810	1855	2100
Grange Bridge		0830	0930	0955	1015	1035	1100	1130	1200	1245	1330	1415	1435	1455	1515	1545	1615	1635	1655	1715	1745	1815	1900	2105
Rosthwaite		0840	0940	1005	1025	1045	1110	1140	1210	1255	1340	1425	1445	1505	1525	1555	1625	1645	1705	1725	1755	1825	1910	2115
Seatoller	0720	0845	0945	1010	1030	1050	1115	1145	1215	1300	1345	1430	1450	1510	1530	1600	1630	1650	1710	1730	1800	1830	1915	2120
Seatoller	0720	0845	0950	1020	1040	1100	1125	1155	1225	1310	1350	1440	1500	1520	1540	1610	1640	1700	1720	1735	1805	1840	1915	2120
Rosthwaite	0724	0850	0955	1025	1045	1105	1130	1200	1230	1315	1355	1445	1505	1525	1545	1615	1645	1705	1725	1740	1810	1845	1920	2125
Grange Bridge	0733	0900	1005	1035	1055	1115	1140	1210	1240	1325	1405	1455	1515	1535	1555	1625	1655	1715	1735	1750	1820	1855	1930	2135
Lodore Hotel	0737	0905	1010	1040	1100	1120	1145	1215	1245	1330	1410	1500	1520	1540	1600	1630	1700	1720	1740	1755	1825	1900	1935	2140
Keswick	0745	0915	1020	1050	1110	1130	1155	1225	1255	1340	1420	1510	1530	1550	1610	1640	1710	1730	1750	1805	1835	1910	1945	2150

The Borrowdale Bus

ECW-bodied Bristol MW No. 231 is shown heading up the Borrowdale Valley from Keswick towards Seatoller. On withdrawal this bus was purchased by a 15 year old schoolboy, Richard Solyom, for preservation. It is now owned by Cumbria Omnibus Group. (HPC)

Leyland National B type No. 810 was painted in this attractive livery of green and cream and given the name 'The Borrowdale Bus' with route details on the side. It is shown leaving Keswick on a very pleasant Autumn morning in October 1994.

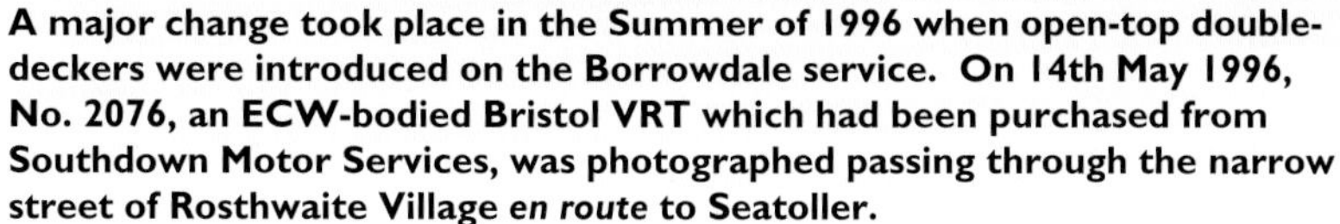

A major change took place in the Summer of 1996 when open-top double-deckers were introduced on the Borrowdale service. On 14th May 1996, No. 2076, an ECW-bodied Bristol VRT which had been purchased from Southdown Motor Services, was photographed passing through the narrow street of Rosthwaite Village *en route* to Seatoller.

On 18th August 1997, Bristol VRT No. 2076 arrives at Seatoller from Keswick showing the cycle rack attached to the rear.

A complete change of environment for Northern Counties-bodied Leyland Olympian No. 2117, B117 TVU. It was new to GM Buses and spent its earlier life plying the streets of Manchester. Following transfer within the Stagecoach Group it was converted to open-top and is shown leaving Seatoller for Keswick.

Displaying the later livery with a greater area of cream and also Stagecoach fleet names, Leyland Olympian No. 2145 leaves Keswick bus station for Seatoller in August 2002. Alongside is MAN No. 801 awaiting departure to Penrith on service X50 whilst an Olympian on service 555 is in the background.

Showing the green Lakes version of the standard Stagecoach livery, Volvo Olympian No. 16329 was photographed at Seatoller on 26th August 2010. (RD)

The Honister Rambler

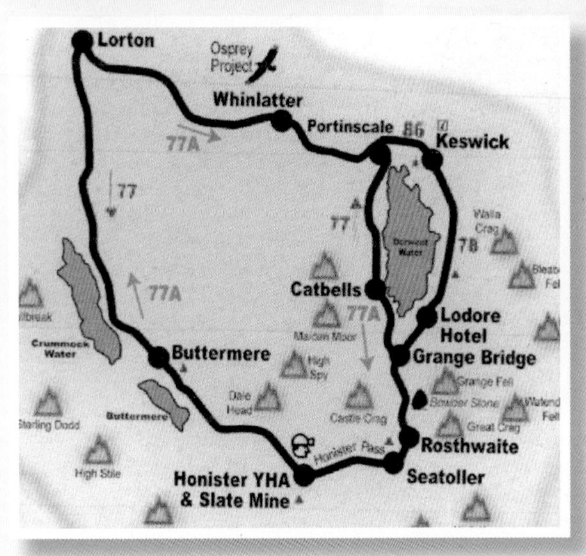

The Honister Rambler is a circular service operating from Keswick via Whinlatter and Honister Passes. It operates in Spring, Summer and Autumn in both directions as services 77 and 77A. In September 1996 minibus No. 78 was just arriving at the summit of Honister Pass from the Borrowdale side operating service 77A. A condition of the granting of the licence was that the vehicles be fitted with retarders.

Crossing the bridge at Grange in Borrowdale in May 1996 in order to return to Keswick on service 77 along the west side of Derwentwater is No. 78.

In 2010 two specially designed Optare Solos with larger wheels and revised front and rear skirts were introduced to replace the Mercedes minibuses; numbered 47721 and 47722, the latter is seen leaving Keswick bus station in August 2010 operating the 13.30hrs departure on service 77A to Buttermere. (RD)

Climbing Honister Pass from the Buttermere side on 18th August 1997 operating service 77 is minibus No 78.

Central Lakeland

Mercedes 608 minibus No. 520, taken over with the South Lakes and Furness areas from Ribble, arrives in Ambleside in September 1993 operating service 506 from Bowness to Coniston. One of the problems with these vehicles was that many of the passengers carried large rucksacks creating an accommodation issue, which led to the introduction of Volvo B6 midibuses on the service.

Volvo B6 No. 276 arrives at Bowness on Windermere in May 2001 on service 505 from Coniston and prepares to turn in readiness for the return journey. To the left hand side of the photograph is an open-top double-decker ready for service 599 to Grasmere.

In typical Lakeland scenery crossing the bridge over the River Rothay at Ambleside in June 2001 and heading for Ambleside and Bowness is Volvo B6 No. 275, carrying 'The Langdale Rambler' name.

With the mountain 'Coniston Old Man' prominent in the background, No. 282 is shown leaving Coniston for Bowness on Windermere on 12th July 1999.

Passing by the side of Yew Tree Tarn between Skelwith Bridge and Coniston on 12th July 1999 and heading for Coniston is No. 275.

Volvo B6 previously numbered 282 but now identified as 30282 in the Stagecoach system is shown leaving Elterwater on 15th November 2007 working the Dungeon Ghyll to Ambleside service with the magnificent Langdale Pikes in the background. (DMcA)

The Central Lakes Open-top Service

Ribble had for many years operated a standard single-deck service between Ambleside and Bowness on Windermere. After Cumberland took over the area, Guide Friday came in with an open-top double-deck service with a day ticket offering unlimited travel. Cumberland countered this with a local service at local individual fares using mainly ex-Southdown Bristol VRT models painted in a green and cream livery. Initially the service operated between Ambleside and Bowness on Windermere but was later extended to and from Grasmere. The photograph shows No. 2037 arriving at Bowness on 14th August 1997.

Olympian No. 2129 passes Nab Cottage, above, as it travels along the side of Rydal Water towards Windermere and Bowness, in June 2001.

Leaving Ambleside for Bowness, left, in September 1997 is Leyland Olympian No. 2102.

Later, Leyland Titans which had started their lives in London were used on the open-top service between Grasmere and Bowness. On 16th June 2003 No. 11110 was photographed having just departed from the Grasmere terminus. Above right is the typically distinctive rear view of Titan No. 10254 at Waterhead, Ambleside on 28th June 2005 with Lake Windermere in the background.

The latest recruits to the open-top service have been Dennis Trident low floor models with Alexander bodies. One of these, No. 17012 is shown arriving in Grasmere on 24th June 2010, passing the bookshop, seen on the corner to the right, with the appropriate name – Sam Read – Bookseller. It sports the latest livery for this service, the green version of the standard Stagecoach livery. (RD)

Here Alexander-bodied Volvo Olympian No. 16294 is shown leaving Ambleside on 19th April 2009. (DMcA)

The 555 – A Scenic Double-Deck Bus Route

Coach-seated Leyland Olympian No. 1001, transferred from West Cumbria to operate on the 555 service, leaves the stop at Thirlspot heading for Lancaster.

In contrasting weather conditions on 14th July 2007, a Volvo Olympian splashes through roadside puddles near Wythburn. (DMcA)

In October 1994, Leyland Olympian No. 1024, above, had descended Dunmail Raise and was approaching Grasmere when photographed with Helm Crag in the left background.

Travelling along the eastern shore of Thirlmere is Alexander-bodied Dennis Trident No. 18358. Clearance of trees along the A591 at this point gave passengers a better view of the lake which for many years has been one of the main sources of water supply for Manchester. It is an interesting point that water travels from here to Manchester entirely by gravity. (DMcA)

With snow-covered mountains in the background, Alexander-bodied Dennis Trident No. 18366 climbs away from Windermere Station in this spectacular view taken on 30th January 2010. (DMcA)

In bright conditions on 2nd September 2002, Volvo Olympian No. 2284 was photographed at Grasmere heading for Lancaster, but on the 556 variation of the route.

On 28th June 2005, Volvo Olympian No. 16331 was photographed heading south at Low Wood just south of Ambleside and with Lake Windermere visible on the left.

Journey's end. On 15th June 2000 Leyland Olympian No. 1026 arrives in Lancaster and having crossed Skerton Bridge, is just a few minutes away from Lancaster bus station.

Contrasting weather conditions can make for good pictures as comparison with the illustration at the top left of this page shows. On a rather damp and dismal day, 5th January 2008, Dennis Trident No. 18359 leaves Grasmere, below, just a little further along the same road, heading towards the A591 road to continue its journey to Lancaster. (DMcA)

Special Lakeland Liveries

When the Dennis Tridents arrived from Stagecoach Manchester, agreement was reached with Cumbria Tourism for some to be painted in special liveries, relating to the Lake District, the cost of painting being shared equally between Cumbria Tourism and Stagecoach.

Heading into Keswick, top, and displaying the *William Wordsworth – Poetry in Motion* livery is No. 18356. Due to town centre road works, it had been diverted via the A66 and Crosthwaite. (DMcA)

Displaying the livery of the well-known Lakeland character, *Peter Rabbit*, No. 18354 sweeps along the shores of Thirlmere on 25th May 2008 on service 555 to Lancaster. (DMcA)

An early morning view of No. 18357 in the *Lakeland Pathfinder* livery as it passes through Kendal operating from Holme to Keswick on 24th June 2010. (RD)

In addition to the Tridents, other vehicles have carried special liveries relating to the Lake District. Plaxton Beaver 2-bodied Mercedes 0814D No. 42545 was loading in Keswick on 10th May 2008 with *Osprey Bus* vinyls for the service to Dodd Wood and Whinlatter Forest the area of England's only nesting Ospreys. (DMcA)

National Express

From Summer 1981 Cumberland participated on a regular basis on the Whitehaven to London service and Duple-bodied Leyland Leopard No. 620 is shown leaving Keswick for Whitehaven on 1st June 1981.

A Saturdays only service was operated by Cumberland from Whitehaven to Blackpool and later became part of the National Express network as indicated here with No. 615, having arrived in Blackpool, and displaying service No. 919 in August 1983. A young lady on the front seat seems to be taking great care of her doll and eyeing the photographer with suspicion.

Eastern Coach Works-bodied Leyland Leopard No. 638 had just left Preston bus station, returning from London to Whitehaven when photographed in April 1984.

PRESTON
SHEFFIELD
STRANRAER

Approaching Preston bus station on the return journey from Nottingham to Whitehaven on 24th July 1986 is Alexander-bodied Leyland Tiger No. 646. (RD)

Two views of Duple Laser-bodied Leyland Tiger No. 106 showing it far from home. The front nearside view shows it in Uttoxeter in July 1985 returning from Nottingham on service 952. The front offside view (photo MB) shows it leaving Peterborough bus station on 31st December 1987 operating service 351 from Cambridge to Whitehaven.

Displaying the 'Rapide' version of National Express livery is No. 107 as it speeds (legally) along the A591 when operating the Rapide service from Whitehaven to London in September 1985. After arrival at London Victoria Coach Station it would operate the London to Minehead National Express service.

EXETER
GLASGOW
INVERNESS

Cross-country journeys do not get much more cross-country than Whitehaven to Lowestoft. Former 'Rapide' coach No. 108 was operating on this service on a hazy morning of 6th June 1992 when photographed leaving Keswick bus station. It was carrying the 'Coachline' livery based on the former Yeowart's colours and was probably being used because of the non-availability of a National Express-liveried coach.

With a long journey ahead of it, Plaxton-bodied Leyland Tiger 'Expressliner' No. 121 leaves Workington Bus station *en route* from Whitehaven to London on 29th September 1993.

By Cumberland coach to Aberdeen. Plaxton-bodied Volvo B10M No. 128 (N128 VAO) arrives at Forton Services on the M6 for driver changeover on 27th September 1995. The previous day it would have operated the Whitehaven to London service, and now it was operating the London to Aberdeen service. It would return to London the following day and then operate from London to Whitehaven the day after. Mileage was clearly considerable and maintenance needed to be *par excellence*.

Pulling into Windermere Station on 18th July 2002 is Jonckheere-bodied Volvo B10M No. 134 showing a later version of the 'Rapide' livery operating service 570 to London. With effect from November 2005 Cumberland ceased operation of National Express services, the contract for the Whitehaven to London service passing to another operator.

Cumberland in Lancashire

With effect from 1st February 1997, Stagecoach transferred operations in North Lancashire, centred on Lancaster and Morecambe, to Cumberland Motor Services. The name Stagecoach Lancaster was adopted. The reasons behind this, together with further information on transport in Morecambe and Lancaster, are given in the author's book 'Morecambe and Lancaster' published by Venture Publications in 2011.

Entering Lancaster City Centre on 30th April 1997 is ex-Ribble Leyland Olympian No. 2207. Ribble, unlike Cumberland, had retained the double line destination display on these vehicles.

Leaving North Road and heading for the bus station in Lancaster in September 2001 is an Alexander-bodied Volvo B10M which had been transferred from the original Cumberland fleet.

Volvo B6 No. 275 in Lakeland livery had rambled quite a long way from home when photographed on Morecambe Promenade on 6th April 2000, operating a local service whilst on loan to White Lund Depot.

Plaxton-bodied Leyland Tiger No. 109 is shown leaving Preston bus station on 6th March 2000 carrying the later version of the Coachline livery of deep red with gold lettering. It was returning to Morecambe from Southport on Service X51 and was now carrying the 'cherished' registration number WLT 706. When new it had, with sister vehicle No. 110, been based at Whitehaven and operated on National Express Services. Both vehicles were fitted with an early form of electronic destination display which was far from satisfactory – hence the use of a paper label carrying the service number and destination.

An open-top service was introduced between Happy Mount Park and Heysham Village in the Summer of 1997 and Leyland Olympian No. 2102 in Lakeland livery is shown arriving at Heysham Village on 18th August 1997. The service, which brought back green liveried buses to Morecambe, was not repeated in the following years.

A low-floor Alexander-bodied MAN emerges from North Road, Lancaster heading for the bus station on 1st August 2001.

Standing in Morecambe bus station awaiting departure to Preston is Alexander-bodied Scania 15297 on 16th April 2011. (MB)

Symbolic of the British Summer weather, these three photographs, taken in Lancaster on 2nd August 2011 in sunshine, were taken only a couple of hours after those taken in Carlisle in wet and miserable conditions and shown on page 68.

A Dennis Trident is shown above coming to the end of North Road before turning into Damside Street for the bus station.

An example of the ever-present Optare Solo, No. 47017 emerges from Chapel Street and crosses North Road.

An ADL Enviro, No. 27744, passes the junction of Chapel Street and North Road as it heads to the bus station.

Personalities

The history of a company such as Cumberland Motor Services is more than a history of vehicles and services, it is also about people who made it all possible. A few of those people are shown in these photographs.

Anne Gloag presents the late Douglas Haig with an award to mark his 35 years service with the company. Douglas was a Whitehaven man who knew the town and its people, together with their requirements for bus services very well. He was the custodian of the company photographs and memorabilia and the author very much appreciated his help and encouragement when writing the two previous books on the company. (CMS)

A photograph taken at Windermere in August 1982 on the occasion of the annual Luncheon for employees with 40 or more years service and to which the author was invited. Peter Townley the General Manager at the time is second from the right whilst at the extreme left is the late Gerry Carruthers who rose through the company to become Assistant Chief Engineer. To his left is the late Algie Corlett who retired as Works Superintendent having joined the company in the 'twenties. The gentleman with the white hair in the centre of the back row is the late Arthur Cowin, son of George Cowin, one of the original directors. The late Jim Weekes was Chief Engineer at the time and is shown third from the right at the back. (CMS)

This photograph is dated 'late 1997' and shows a selection of staff with Messrs Barry Hinkley and Les Warneford. (CMS)